IMPROVING
FEDERAL PROGRAM
PERFORMANCE

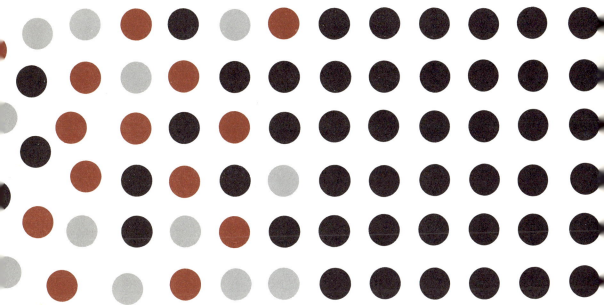

A Statement on National Policy
by the Research and Policy Committee
of the Committee for Economic Development
September 1971

Single Copy ... $1.50

Printed in U.S.A.
First Printing September 1971
Design: Harry Carter
Library of Congress Catalog Card Number: 70-173676

Committee for Economic Development
477 Madison Avenue, New York, N.Y. 10022

Contents

THE RESPONSIBILITY FOR
CED STATEMENTS ON NATIONAL POLICY

This statement has been approved for publication as a statement of the Research and Policy Committee by the members of that Committee and its drafting subcommittee, subject to individual dissents or reservations noted herein. The trustees who are responsible for this statement are listed on the opposite page. Company associations are included for identification only; the companies do not share in the responsibility borne by the individuals.

The Research and Policy Committee is directed by CED's bylaws to:

"Initiate studies into the principles of business policy and of public policy which will foster the full contribution by industry and commerce to the attainment and maintenance of high and secure standards of living for people in all walks of life through maximum employment and high productivity in the domestic economy."

The bylaws emphasize that:

"All research is to be thoroughly objective in character, and the approach in each instance is to be from the standpoint of the general welfare and not from that of any special political or economic group."

The Research and Policy Committee is composed of 50 Trustees from among the 200 businessmen and educators who comprise the Committee for Economic Development. It is aided by a Research Advisory Board of leading economists, a small permanent Research Staff, and by advisors chosen for their competence in the field being considered.

Each Statement on National Policy is preceded by discussions, meetings, and exchanges of memoranda, often stretching over many months. The research is undertaken by a subcommittee, with its advisors, and the full Research and Policy Committee participates in the drafting of findings and recommendations.

Except for the members of the Research and Policy Committee and the responsible subcommittee, the recommendations presented herein are not necessarily endorsed by other Trustees or by the advisors, contributors, staff members, or others associated with CED.

The Research and Policy Committee offers these Statements on National Policy as an aid to clearer understanding of the steps to be taken in achieving sustained growth of the American economy. The Committee is not attempting to pass on any pending specific legislative proposals; its purpose is to urge careful consideration of the objectives set forth in the statement and of the best means of accomplishing those objectives.

4.

5.

PROJECT DIRECTOR

FRED S. HOFFMAN
Los Angeles, California

ADVISORS TO THE SUBCOMMITTEE

JACK W. CARLSON
Assistant Director for Program Evaluation
Office of Management and Budget
Executive Office of the President

ARNOLD HARBERGER
Department of Economics
University of Chicago

JOHN R. MEYER
President
National Bureau of Economic
Research, Inc.

FREDERICK C. MOSHER
Woodrow Wilson Department of
Government and Foreign Affairs
University of Virginia

ANDREW M. ROUSE
Deputy Executive Director
President's Advisory Council on
Executive Organization
Executive Office of the President

DONALD C. STONE
Graduate School of Public and
International Affairs
University of Pittsburgh

SEYMOUR L. WOLFBEIN
Dean, School of Business Administration
Temple University

CED Staff Advisors
SOL HURWITZ
FRANK W. SCHIFF
ROBERT F. STEADMAN

RESEARCH ADVISORY BOARD

Chairman
CHARLES L. SCHULTZE
The Brookings Institution

EDWARD C. BANFIELD
Department of Government
Harvard University

ALAN K. CAMPBELL
Dean, The Maxwell School of Citizenship
and Public Affairs
Syracuse University

WILBUR J. COHEN
Dean, School of Education
The University of Michigan

WALTER W. HELLER
Department of Economics
University of Minnesota

LAWRENCE C. HOWARD
Dean, Graduate School of Public
and International Affairs
University of Pittsburgh

CARL KAYSEN
Director, The Institute for Advanced Study
Princeton University

JOHN R. MEYER
President
National Bureau of Economic Research,Inc.

FREDERICK C. MOSHER
Woodrow Wilson Department of
Government and Foreign Affairs
University of Virginia

DON K. PRICE
Dean, John Fitzgerald Kennedy School
of Government
Harvard University

RAYMOND VERNON
Graduate School
of Business Administration
Harvard University

HENRY C. WALLICH
Department of Economics
Yale University

Associate Members
CHARLES P. KINDLEBERGER
Department of Economics and Social Science
Massachusetts Institute of Technology

MITCHELL SVIRIDOFF
Vice President, Division of National Affairs
The Ford Foundation

PAUL N. YLVISAKER
Professor, Public Affairs and
Urban Planning
Woodrow Wilson School of Public
and International Affairs
Princeton University

6.

FOREWORD

Improving the process by which federal programs are developed, financed, and managed is a challenging task. The complex nature of our political system and the stubborn resistance to change inherent in a giant governmental bureaucracy pose formidable obstacles. Nevertheless, the magnitude of federal spending for public programs—totalling an estimated $230 billion or about 22 per cent of the gross national product in the current fiscal year—makes such improvement essential for defining the optimum level of those expenditures and for getting the most out of the money spent. Rising expenditures for grants-in-aid to state and local governments, and for new social programs with benefits that are difficult to measure in dollar terms, only intensify the need for assuring better program performance.

The process by which the federal government employs and manages resources has been a continuing concern of this Committee, and a number of earlier CED policy statements are directly related to this statement on *Improving Federal Program Performance.* A 1964 statement, *Improving Executive Management in the Federal Government,* called attention to the selection, development, and compensation of career executives in government. *Budgeting for National Objectives* (1966) examined the use of the federal budget as an instrument for defining and achieving national goals and objectives. *Making Congress More Effective* (1970) highlighted the structural and procedural weaknesses that impair the effectiveness of the Legislative Branch.

The present statement is somewhat more technical than previous works. In preparing it we were fortunate to be able to draw on the first-hand experience and specialized knowledge of CED trustees and advisers who have spent many years in government service. The statement focuses attention on three major areas of concern about federal programs: first, the choice of policy goals and program objectives; second, the selection of programs that will achieve those objectives; and, finally, the execution

7.

of programs and the evaluation of their performance to determine the extent to which their stated objectives are being achieved in fact. Implicit in the changes recommended in the statement is the need for greater accountability by government to the people. Accordingly, the report urges the President to make a major commitment on behalf of his Administration to increase accountability in the federal government. Specifically, it calls for public disclosure of more adequate information on the goals of government policies and the cost and effectiveness of government programs in achieving their objectives. Only when such information is available will citizens be able to make informed judgments about how well their tax dollars are being spent.

Improving Federal Program Performance was prepared by a subcommittee headed by Marvin Bower. The project director was Fred S. Hoffman, a former Assistant Director of the U.S. Bureau of the Budget. I would like to extend the appreciation of the Research and Policy Committee to Mr. Bower, Mr. Hoffman, and to members and advisers of the subcommittee for their important contributions to this project. I would also like to make special mention of the valuable assistance of Robert W. Fri of the Washington office of McKinsey & Company, who is now on leave as Deputy Administrator of the Environmental Protection Agency, and to P. Jackson Bell, also of the Washington office of McKinsey & Company.

CED studies in the area of Improvement of Management in Government, which includes this statement, are supported by grants from the Carnegie Corporation, the Rockefeller Brothers Fund, the Kellogg Foundation, and other foundations and donors whose assistance we acknowledge with gratitude.

Emilio G. Collado, *Co-Chairman*
Research and Policy Committee

1 Introduction and Summary of Recommendations

$\mathbf{T}$he notion of inefficiency in the federal government is well established in the popular mind.[1] Even Presidents share this view of government. Yet voters, Congressmen, and Presidents continually act to increase the federal establishment's activities and responsibilities. Resolving the paradox of the government's present level of effectiveness and its growing assignments has become a vital national issue.*

THE ROLE OF PROGRAMS

The chief means for the conduct of federal activities are "programs"—or groups of related activities designed to achieve specific objectives. The federal government establishes, finances, and manages an enormous number of programs in pursuit of our national goals.[2] Federal programs are vast in scope—ranging from housing and health to national defense and international affairs. And they are costly to carry out. In the fiscal year 1972 the federal government will spend an estimated $230 billion or about 22 per cent of the gross national product (GNP) on public programs. In future years the nation will require additional and expanded programs if we are to make progress in rebuilding the cities, cleaning up the environment, improving education, and achieving other important national goals.

Yet the federal government lacks adequate means for establishing and executing programs and for evaluating the contributions that they

[1]/The notion is so well established that it has been a frequent subject of humorous writing in the nation's press. For an example, see Appendix A.

[2]/In this statement, "goal" is used to mean long-term mission or direction for public policy while "objective" is used to mean a sub-goal designed to advance toward the goal. Thus, in the President's message on the postal service, setting up the postal service as an authority was given as an "objective" for achieving the "goal of the best postal service in the world."

*See Memoranda by MR. JOHN D. HARPER, page 63, and by MR. FRANKLIN A. LINDSAY, page 64.

9.

make to society relative to their cost. It lacks adequate means for creating inducements and incentives for improving its performance in executing these programs. And it lacks adequate means for assuring coordination and cooperation with state and local levels of government, where federal domestic programs are being increasingly conducted.

The federal government can afford neither to ignore costs nor to engage in arbitrary budget cutting, without jeopardizing the national welfare. Faced with this dilemma, it is essential that it improve the ways in which it uses programs to allocate and employ resources. We believe that this improvement can be achieved through better performance of the following five basic steps:

1. *Formulating Program Goals and Objectives.* We cannot move reliably and effectively toward a particular goal without a clear concept of what that goal is and of the specific objectives that must be achieved on the way. Public policy goals in our society do not attempt to define in detail the quality of life. They seek instead to establish a framework within which individual choice is broadened and private ends are more easily achieved. Under our democratic form of government, the goals of public policy must be developed, specified, and ratified by the political process as an expression of the people's will. But in order for that will to result in effective action, government officials and the public at large must participate in a continuing process of self-education. Objectives and even goals must be revised as more is learned about their costs and interrelationships.

2. *Choosing Among Alternatives.* Decisions on how to achieve objectives should involve a choice among significantly different alternate courses of action. Unless such alternatives are considered, programs will not stay attuned to changing objectives and priorities, nor will there be a proper balance between cost and effectiveness. Estimates of cost and effectiveness should be based on a real and specific understanding of the process by which the goods or services involved are to be produced. Particularly in the newer program areas, valid analysis of alternative programs requires fundamental research and experimentation on relationships between means and ends, results and costs.

3. *Translating Program Decisions into a Plan for Execution.* After individual program choices are made, all programs must be combined into a feasible plan for the operating bureau, the agency, and the federal government, together with an over-all operating budget. For each

10.

program the plan should establish a budget of resources and objectives for the operating period, against which to test program performance. Since most program activities have output or cost implications that extend significantly beyond the federal government's one-year operating and budgeting period, the total cost and output implications for future years should be shown for program decisions in the budget years.

4. *Executing the Program.* Once a plan has been developed, people must carry it out. The responsible officials must have the will to manage; and they must have the leadership and executive ability to make that will effective on a day-to-day operating basis. They must instill a determination to get results, an impatience with delays, and a consciousness of costs. These essential ingredients are not matters of method but the results of careful selection of competent personnel and appropriate assignment of responsibility. In both areas the President himself must exert strong leadership. And, of course, even competent personnel require training and direction.

5. *Monitoring Program Execution.* Effective program evaluation is the basis for accountability in government, as well as a necessary check on the validity of the planning process and management effectiveness. Program evaluation is necessary to strengthen the incentives and inducements for responsive and effective management of public programs and thus protect them against political expediency. Two basically different kinds of evaluation are needed. First, the measurement of program results against the objectives for which the program was established and funded should become a regular responsibility of program managers. Second, more intensive evaluations of program performance and goals are required occasionally to support major decisions about initiating new programs, reorienting existing programs, or renewing the authorizations of a particularly important program. To support both kinds of evaluation, operating plans should include a plan for collecting data and other information.

* * *

Clearly, these five steps suggest a rational and orderly process that is far from being realized. But we believe that these fundamentals in some form are essential in improving program performance. We are aware, however, that achievement of this level of effectiveness must be evolutionary and cannot be attained by the abrupt imposition of any formal system.

SCOPE OF THIS STATEMENT

The focus of this statement is primarily on programs of the federal government, and the processes of developing, executing, and evaluating them. By its very nature this process is related to the over-all level of government spending and revenues, but because this subject has been dealt with at some length in recent CED statements,[3] it is treated here only peripherally.

Although our emphasis is on domestic programs, much of our discussion is relevant to national security programs as well. In fact, the procedures of the Department of Defense have served as a model for past attempts to reform resource allocation and management methods in other parts of the federal establishment. Still, there are important differences beween domestic and national security programs which we will not explore here. The special nature of the national security process is under study by this Committee, and will be discussed in a forthcoming CED statement.

Our decision to concentrate in this statement on federal programs does not imply a lower priority for improving the performance of state and local governments. Indeed, the bulk of domestic government programs are run by state and local governments,[4] and most federal programs require a substantial amount of intergovernmental coordination and cooperation. These points were underscored in earlier statements by this Committee calling for sweeping renovations in the structure and processes of state, metropolitan, and local governments.[5] The rising proportion of federal spending devoted to grants-in-aid indicates that federal domestic programs are increasingly conducted at lower levels of government where decentralized "delivery systems" can be more flexible and more responsive to varying local needs (see Figures 1 and 2). With grants-in-aid to state and local governments mounting rapidly and with revenue sharing being advocated as a means of strengthening state and local fiscal resources, there is good reason to apply the principles set forth in this statement to state and municipal programs.

---

[3]/*Further Weapons Against Inflation* (November 1970) and *Fiscal and Monetary Policies for Steady Economic Growth* (January 1969), Statements on National Policy by the Research and Policy Committee, Committee for Economic Development.

[4]/For relative magnitudes of state-local and federal program operations, see Appendix B.

[5]/*Modernizing Local Government* (July 1966), *A Fiscal Program for a Balanced Federalism* (June 1967), *Modernizing State Government* (July 1967), and *Reshaping Government in Metropolitan Areas* (February 1970), Statements on National Policy by the Research and Policy Committee, Committee for Economic Development.

Figure 1: GNP AND THE COMPOSITION OF FEDERAL SPENDING *(in billions of dollars)*

Fiscal Year	GNP	Purchase of Goods and Services		Domestic Transfer Payments	Grants-in-aid to State and Local Governments	Other*	Total
		Defense	Nondefense				
1972e	n.a.	74.0	28.2	72.5	34.4	21.0	230.1
1971e	1012	74.1	23.8	67.0	27.0	23.1	215.0
1968	827	75.8	19.4	42.4	17.6	17.1	172.3
1965	654	48.9	15.5	28.3	10.9	14.9	118.5
1960	495	45.1	7.9	20.8	6.9	10.9	91.1
1955	379	38.6	5.3	12.1	3.0	8.3	67.4
1950	263	12.6	6.3	11.3	2.4	9.7	42.4

e *Estimate*
n.a. *Not available*

Includes foreign transfer payments, net interest paid, net subsidies of government enterprises, and net wage accruals.

Source: *Data from U.S. Office of Management and Budget,* The Budget of the United States Government, Fiscal Year 1972 *(Washington, D.C.: U.S. Government Printing Office, 1971), pp. 574-575.*

Figure 2: THE COMPOSITION OF FEDERAL SPENDING *(percentage of total spending)*

Fiscal Year	Purchase of Goods and Services		Domestic Transfer Payments	Grants-in-aid to State and Local Governments	Other	Total
	Defense	Nondefense				
1972	32	12	31	15	10	100
1971	34	11	31	13	11	100
1968	44	11	24	10	11	100
1965	42	14	24	9	11	100
1960	50	9	23	8	10	100
1955	57	8	18	5	12	100
1950	30	15	27	6	22	100

Source: *Data from U.S. Office of Management and Budget,* Special Analyses, Budget of the United States Government, Fiscal Year 1972, *pp. 20-21.*

13.

Nevertheless, there are valid reasons for centering attention on improving program performance at the federal level. The federal government is the largest single governmental entity and the one in which the decision-making apparatus is most highly centralized. As we indicated earlier, in the fiscal year 1972 the federal government will spend an estimated $230 billion or about 22 per cent of GNP on public programs.

Moreover, the federal government exerts influence on both the procedures and substance of state and local governments in three important ways: (1) It is a growing source of revenue for state and local governments. There are currently some $30 billion in federal grant-in-aid programs that need evaluation by the federal government, working in cooperation with states and localities. (2) Federal decisions affect the size and—through specification of purpose in categorical and bloc grants—the content of state and local programs. In this way the federal government has been an important force for innovation in programs to be operated at state and local levels. (3) In adopting administrative reforms, strengthening executive capability, and improving management practices and techniques, the federal government often sets the example for state and local governments.

CONDITIONS
AFFECTING PROGRAM PERFORMANCE

In considering the challenge of improving the performance of federal programs, two basic conditions must be borne in mind. First, a major portion of the federal budget is already committed to existing programs. Second, improved performance must be effected under political conditions.

Control Limitations

Although the federal government spends billions of dollars on public programs, a large proportion of these outlays are relatively uncontrollable under present laws. An estimated $152.2 billion—or about two-thirds of the total budget for the fiscal year 1972—is devoted to relatively uncontrollable outlays (see Figure 3). While the Congress has the power to change the laws that govern these outlays, at present less than one-fifth of total spending can be assigned to domestic programs whose levels are not prescribed by existing authorizing legislation.

14.

Figure 3: CONTROLLABILITY OF BUDGET OUTLAYS *(in billions of dollars)*

	1970 actual	1971 estimate	1972 estimate
Relatively uncontrollable outlays under present law:			
Open-ended programs and fixed costs:			
Social insurance trust funds:			
Social security trust funds	30.3	34.4	35.9
Medicare trust funds	7.1	8.3	9.4
Unemployment trust funds	3.6	6.0	5.2
Retirement and other trust funds	4.2	4.9	5.3
Subtotal, social insurance trust funds	**45.2**	**53.6**	**55.8**
Interest	18.3	19.4	19.7
Veterans benefits: Pensions, compensation, education, and insurance	6.6	7.8	8.4
Medicaid program	2.7	3.3	3.8
Other public assistance grants	4.7	6.4	7.6
Farm price supports (Commodity Credit Corp.)	3.8	3.2	3.6
Food stamp program	.6	1.5	2.0
Military retired pay	2.8	3.4	3.7
Postal Service	1.5	2.4	1.3
Legislative and Judiciary	.5	.5	.6
Other	2.1	2.9	3.6
Outlays from prior-year contracts and obligations:			
National defense	24.9	22.4	22.4
Civilian programs	16.6	19.2	19.6
Subtotal, relatively uncontrollable outlays	**130.2**	**146.0**	**152.2**
Allowance for pay raises:			
Department of Defense	....	.9	2.4
Civilian agencies	....	.5	1.0
Relatively controllable outlays:			
National defense:			
Proposed volunteer army program	....	....	1.2
Other	52.3	49.6	47.8
Civilian programs:			
Proposed added amounts for revenue sharing	....	....	4.0
Proposed social security benefit increase	....	1.1	3.0
Other	20.5	21.5	24.5
Allowance for contingencies	....	.3	1.0
Undistributed intragovernmental transactions	—6.4	—7.2	—7.8
Total budget outlays	**196.6**	**212.8**	**229.2**

Source: U.S. Office of Management and Budget, The Budget of the United States Government, Fiscal Year 1972, *p. 527.*

15.

This analysis highlights the fact that present laws which automatically commit funds to existing programs significantly limit control over the allocation of resources. In view of this limitation, it is all the more important that attention be given to increasing the effectiveness of newly-inaugurated programs. Moreover, after proper evaluations, changes should be made in existing programs that are found to be inadequate; existing programs for which the need is not well-established should be cut back or discontinued.

Political Realities

To be realistic, the difficulties in achieving substantial improvements in federal program performance are formidable. The barriers that stand in the way of change are deeply rooted in the pluralistic nature of our political process and in the motivations and incentives that govern the behavior of elected and appointed government officials. A simplistic approach to the problem that ignores these facts has little chance for success; on the contrary, it can make matters significantly worse.

The changes suggested in this statement imply greater accountability by government to the people in allocating and managing resources through programs. As the trend toward public involvement in government increases—not only in the formulations of goals for public action but more directly in the operations of public programs—a fundamental condition for improved program performance is a public that is well-informed on both procedural and substantive issues. In a speech advocating increased and more effective economic education in the schools, a leading business executive once put it this way: "if we have enough voters totally ignorant of [the] pros and cons, they can vote the country down the drain without even knowing it."[6] A well-informed public becomes even more important, with the recent addition to the electorate of 18 to 21-year-old men and women.

However, more and better information about the implications of public policies and programs will not eliminate conflict among diverse individual interests. Nor should it. In some cases it may even exacerbate it. Still, we believe that well-informed citizens—making their voices heard through the political process—represent the best assurance that conflict among diverse interests can be resolved. In fact, the increasingly frequent

6/Frederick R. Kappel, "Communications and Change," speech at Economic Education Workshop, Joint Council on Economic Education, Little Rock, Ark. (August 5, 1965).

veto of public actions by special interests can be dealt with not by avoiding politics but by elevating the level of political participation in policy decisions.

ATTEMPTS AT REFORM

Earlier attempts at reform underscore the difficulties of upgrading federal program performance. In 1965 President Johnson announced the Planning-Programming-Budgeting System (PPBS) for the federal government, and in a 1966 policy statement, *Budgeting for National Objectives,* the CED Research and Policy Committee supported the objectives of that system.[7] PPBS was an attempt to review program objectives and consider major program issues in terms of alternative courses of action. This Committee urged the extension of the President's initiative to include improved operational management of programs, more effective budgetary execution, and more intensive review of agency performance.

The Planning-Programming-Budgeting System has often been discussed as though it were a single, well-defined system based on sophisticated techniques of analysis and intended to produce an optimal plan of government activity. The facts have been quite different both as to intent and results. Differences in the functions of agencies and their relations with Congress and in the backgrounds and personalities of agency heads made it inevitable that the system would develop unevenly. Some agencies built large staffs of highly trained analysts—for example, the Department of Defense, where an earlier version of the system was developed, and the Department of Health, Education, and Welfare. Others, such as the Department of Justice, did not. In many cases, PPBS was conducted outside of established budget channels which created competition and confusion.

Despite this unevenness, the 1965 initiative did increase the amount of federal program analysis. The annual requirement to consider major program issues focused more comprehensive and systematic attention on the relation between agency objectives and agency activities. Program analysis and evaluation staffs, established both in the agencies and in the Executive Office of the President, can be expected to continue promoting the comprehensive analysis of federal programs.

7/*Budgeting for National Objectives,* A Statement on National Policy by the Research and Policy Committee, Committee for Economic Development (January 1966).

However, some of the more important problems that PPBS was intended to solve still require considerable attention. These problems are:

- *The stated objectives of government programs are often vague, internally inconsistent, and unrelated to program choice.*

- *Many program choices are made without reference to alternatives.*

- *Information on the cost and effectiveness of proposed programs is often lacking or unreliable.*

- *The development of program budgeting and long-range comprehensive planning is still rudimentary and far from integrated into the resource allocation process.*

- *Evaluation of the actual cost and effectiveness of federal programs is often lacking or invalid.*

SUMMARY OF RECOMMENDATIONS

The recommendations contained in the subsequent chapters of this policy statement highlight three major areas of concern about federal government programs: (1) setting objectives and measuring results, (2) selecting programs to achieve objectives, and (3) program execution and performance evaluation. Together these are essential for prudent distribution and utilization of resources. Although our recommendations are directed toward better performance by the federal government, the principles we have set forth should have considerable relevance not only to state and local governments, as we noted earlier, but also to business, education, and other institutions in the private sector.

The recommendations call for action from federal officials in their capacities as representatives of the people, as creators of policy, and as managers of the public enterprise. But full realization of the intended changes will occur only in a political atmosphere that is conducive to more effective and efficient government. Citizen pressure and influence can help to create that atmosphere. Concerted efforts to support better management of the public's business must be made by business and educational organizations, civic and professional groups—indeed, by every citizen and taxpayer.

18.

1. *Setting Objectives and Measuring Results.* In our pluralistic government process with its complex relationships among the President, the Executive Branch, and the Congress, choices of policy goals and program objectives tend to be political acts. Public understanding of the substance of policy issues and the cost and effectiveness of programs are therefore important if the process is to work well.[8] It may be essential when the public is fragmented over a given issue by deeply-held differences of views or competing interests. Increased accountability is needed, not only to enhance the responsiveness of government but to heighten its effectiveness. The development of public pressure toward this end is a central purpose of this statement.

● **We urge that the President make a major commitment on behalf of his Administration to increase accountability in the federal government. To this end, we recommend that more adequate information be developed on the goals of government policies and the cost and effectiveness of government programs in achieving their objectives, and that such information be made available to the public.**

● **We recommend that the annual messages of the President be recast to provide a better basis for subsequent program evaluation. The Budget document should review past performance against past objectives, give greater emphasis to stating the specific achievements expected from the major programs supported by the budget submission, and relate major current objectives to a long-range plan leading toward policy goals.**

● **We recommend that the federal government sponsor continuing efforts to devise, improve, and publish measures of social and environmental conditions.**

● **We support the objectives of the President's reorganization plans and urge cooperation between the Executive Branch and the Congress in working out the details of an improved structure for the Executive Departments.**

---

[8]/Recognizing the importance of economic education, the Committee for Economic Development—in cooperation with the Ford Foundation—established in 1949 the Joint Council on Economic Education, an independent organization. The Council's mission is to increase the quantity and improve the quality of economics taught in our schools and colleges.

● **Congress should bring pressure to bear for the development of stronger and more regular evaluation of programs in terms of their objectives.**[9] **We applaud the reforms embodied in the Legislative Reorganization Act of 1970 and urge the Congress to use the strengthened staff resources provided by the Act to obtain more independent evaluation. We further recommend that an appropriate continuing committee of the Congress be assigned responsibility for monitoring and reporting periodically to the public on how the provisions of the Act are being carried out.**

● **We recommend that, in authorizing legislation, Congress adopt the practice of requiring periodic program evaluation and that it authorize funds for this purpose. This is particularly important for grant-in-aid programs, even in cases where the federal government will not take part in the evaluation directly.**

2. Selecting Programs To Achieve Objectives. In developing and selecting government programs that will make the greatest contribution to national goals and objectives, three major improvements should be made: (1) the range of alternatives should be expanded; (2) experimental programs should be better planned and more widely used; and (3) program analysis should be strengthened.

● **We recommend that policy-making officials of the federal government, with Presidential leadership, take an active role in developing and widening the range of program alternatives considered in the course of the resource allocation process.**

● **We recommend that analysis of programs involving government spending consider, where appropriate, alternatives that promote social ends by changing private incentives through user charges, taxes, or regulation of private activities, and that such alternatives be adopted in preference to additional public spending whenever they can achieve equal effectiveness. When tax relief incentives, loan guarantees, or other indirect subsidies are used, their costs, including foregone tax revenues, should be es-**

9/For detailed recommendations concerning the role of Congress in improving the performance of federal programs, see pp. 33-35 of this Statement; and *Making Congress More Effective,* A Statement on National Policy by the Research and Policy Committee, Committee for Economic Development (New York: September 1970).

timated and published both at the inception of the program and on a continuing basis thereafter.

● We recommend that in the analysis of most domestic programs consideration be given to entire or partial reliance on the private sector or state and local governments as alternatives to federal operation of federally-financed programs.

● We recommend that deliberately planned experimental programs be used more often by federal agencies to gather information as a basis for program design, planning, and evaluation. In order to permit flexibility and diversity in experimentation, we urge that the scale of the experiment be no larger than that needed to provide the desired information and test operational feasibility. Funds for evaluation should be included in legislation authorizing experimental programs.

● We recommend that cost-benefit analysis, with benefits as well as costs expressed in dollars, be applied to those program outputs for which market values can be estimated.

● In cases where program objectives include public goods for which it is impossible to establish a market value, we recommend that cost-effectiveness analysis be applied to select the most efficient among a set of alternatives, to display tradeoffs among objectives at equal cost, and, where possible, to suggest new and more efficient alternatives.

● We recommend that the Office of Management and Budget periodically review the discount rate used in cost-benefit studies, and pending the determination of a methodology for estimating the appropriate rate, program costs and benefits should be estimated by using a range of rates with the minimum at least as high as the yield on long-term Treasury bonds.

● We recommend that the Office of Management and Budget issue guidelines clarifying the pricing of goods and services provided by the government and the estimation of costs that enter cost-effectiveness analysis.

21.

• **We recommend that cost estimates reflect program uncertainty by showing "possible high" as well as "expected" estimates in program analysis. We further recommend that more sources of independent cost estimates be developed at policy-making levels, and used to reduce biases toward underestimation of program costs in the resource allocation and program planning process. Unjustifiable cost overruns should be penalized through administrative action and contract terms.**

3. *Program Execution and Performance Evaluation.* Once program goals and objectives have been determined and the planning process has selected the means to achieve them, there must be effective execution of decisions and a monitoring of performance to determine whether policy and plans are in fact being effectively carried out. The budget translates program decisions into a specific allocation of resources. It is the task of evaluation to bring actual program experience to bear on major reviews of policy issues, and to determine whether existing programs are achieving their objectives. In this way evaluation can serve as a basis for future planning and management decisions.

• **As a means for showing how resources are allocated among the various purposes of government, and for displaying the cost of each kind of output produced, we support the objectives of program budgeting and recommend that the federal government continue its development.**

• **We recommend a consolidation of the existing functional and program budget classification systems into a single, government-wide system suitable for displaying program costs and outputs, and that the resulting system be based on data elements that permit aggregation on organization, appropriation, or program lines.**

• **We recommend that the Budget document present a five-year projection by major program categories showing program expenditures for each year implied by the commitments inherent in existing program strategy. Major anticipated program achievements should also be shown over the five-year period as a bench mark for evaluating program performance.**

• **We recommend that the office of the agency head and the Office of Management and Budget take active roles in designing** and coordinating program evaluation plans. We further recommend that they review such plans, their costs, and the performance of program managers in carrying them out as part of the normal program review.

● We recommend that the program objectives and cost estimates on the basis of which a program was funded constitute the criteria for evaluating its performance. The objectives should be adopted only after careful consideration of the incentives they establish for program managers. The suitability of program objectives should be reviewed as an integral part of periodic program review by policy-level officials.

● We recommend that small staffs be maintained to assist policy-making officials in program analysis and evaluation. The government should take a more active role in encouraging the kind of interdisciplinary graduate curricula required for training such staffs. "In-house" staffs should be supplemented by the use of contractual arrangements with outside groups; the government should foster through quasi-governmental organizations the development of professional standards and accountability for such groups.

Setting Objectives:
The Basis for Program Design
and Management

The democratic process provides for a free and open debate over the objectives of federal activities and the results of government programs measured against those objectives. The choice of program objectives is in large part a choice of who is to benefit, by how much, at what cost, and at whose expense. Adoption of a particular objective as a basis for program activities is also, at least implicitly, a collective judgment that the benefits, not usually measurable in dollar terms, are worth the dollar cost of the resources necessary to achieve them. Under our system of government, these judgments are political acts in which the President, the Executive Branch, the Congress, and the public play complex, interrelated, and at times conflicting roles.

One reason for prolonged failure in setting the objectives of a public program may be the diversity of interests involved. For example, the government struggled for years to meet the demand for airport facilities and traffic control—without great success, as most air travellers can testify. With respect to this issue, the public is fragmented into many groups with diverse and often overlapping interests. These groups include air travellers (distinguished by the frequency of travel, income, whether they are on expense accounts, etc.), the commercial airlines, general aviation (distinguished by whether the aircraft is a Piper Cub or an executive jet), people who live close enough to the airport to be affected by landing and takeoff noise, and, finally, the tax-paying public which is called upon to finance needed improvements out of the general revenues unless a sufficient set of user charges can be agreed upon. As a result of failure to resolve conflicts among the various interests, effective action was long delayed. And the situation continued to deteriorate long after the need for action was obvious.

Small groups with special interests have the power to influence policy decisions to their own benefit but often at a cost to society at large. This built-in protection for minorities of the electorate is part of our democratic system by design, not by chance, for in a pluralistic society

24.

we are all in the minority on some issues. When differences are deep and important, the bargaining process will be unavoidably long, painful, and costly to all. Unfortunately, confusion and misunderstanding, resulting from lack of information, can often cloud an issue and produce the same costly results even where there is a basis for resolving differences; for the general interest, if properly understood, can often motivate public action despite opposition by special interest groups. Under these circumstances, a clear and effective representation of the public interest becomes a necessity.

THE PRESIDENT: SPOKESMAN FOR THE GENERAL INTEREST

Advocacy of effectiveness, efficiency, and equity, as much as other causes, requires full-time leadership. That leadership must be found within the government. And within the government, the ultimate responsibility can reside only with the President—not the institutionalized Office of the President, but the individual political leader. Only the President can combine the breadth of official responsibility and authority with the political standing required.

Attempts to improve the governmental process cannot proceed very far on purely technical or administrative grounds, or through the adoption of a formal system that lacks public support. In the final analysis, support for a better governmental process must stem from an understanding of the substance of issues and an insistence that the government produce information and make it available. But the need for information cannot be satisfied merely by increasing the already sizable volume of reports on the administrative and technical details of government programs. The need is for analysis that clarifies the objectives of programs, estimates the cost of achieving them by alternative means, and summarizes the effectiveness and cost of existing programs in achieving their objectives. And while such information has to pass the scrutiny of the expert, it is vital that the major conclusions be intelligible to the general public.

Since information about program cost and effectiveness may prove embarrassing to those involved in the programs, it will often be withheld or not produced if the matter is left to the individual discretion of program managers, agency heads, Congressional committees, or segments of the public that benefit from particular programs. Some pressure

25.

to produce information is generated through adversary proceedings between the Executive Branch and the Congress, or between agencies and the Office of Management and Budget. But public understanding should be reinforced by a Presidential commitment to develop and make *publicly* available information on the implications of government policies and the cost and effectiveness of existing and proposed programs.

President Nixon has often stated his concern with improving the quality of government programs. In the recent reorganization of the Executive Office of the President, he has taken a number of steps to strengthen the process of policy formulation and the quality of program management. A major commitment to supply the public with more adequate information on program objectives and performance is essential for improving incentives for effectiveness and efficiency in government while maintaining the essentially political character of the process. **We urge that the President make a major commitment on behalf of his Administration to increase accountability in the federal government. To this end, we recommend that more adequate information be developed on the goals of government policies and the cost and effectiveness of government programs in achieving their objectives, and that such information be made available to the public.**

Clarifying Goals and Defining Objectives

The delineation and clarification of the goals of government policy are continuing tasks for Presidential leadership. Social purposes change and conflict; so do the resources and techniques available to achieve them. Therefore, it is important for the President and his Administration to review periodically the goals of public programs as a basis for the continuing evaluation of the programs themselves. Such a review should be made a more explicit part of the federal government's resource allocation plan; for unless the plan reflects an orderly process for relating program objectives to policy goals, program managers receive only haphazard guidance from policy levels as to the operational significance of these goals.

More importantly, the absence of a plan that estimates anticipated program costs and states explicit objectives invites program managers to ensure that spending will be no less than the specified level and to rationalize about program achievements. And rationalization is easy, for it is always possible to argue after the fact that a program has done what it

26.

should do when there are no authoritative specifications of objectives. If, on the other hand, anticipated achievements have been specified and explicitly stated during the planning and budgeting process, and revised to reflect the impact of Congressional changes, differences between those objectives and the actual program achievements revealed by the program evaluation process are a proper basis for questions by higher levels of management in the Executive Branch, and by Congress and the public. Such differences need not reflect adversely on the usefulness of a program, but they should not be ignored. Decisions to initiate or to fund a program should therefore be based on specifications of its expected achievements. Subsequent program evaluation should compare actual with anticipated results.

The President's Budget

As this Committee emphasized in *Budgeting for National Objectives,* the President's Budget can contribute significantly to the process of setting goals and objectives and improving the allocation and management of resources. But if the Budget document is to serve as a broad resource allocation plan for the government as well as an instrument for financial control, a number of changes are required. It must specify not only funding requirements but also program objectives to be achieved, and it must do so in terms that serve to guide management and to measure its performance within the budget period. It must also deal with program objectives and costs that extend beyond the single year now covered in the Budget document.

We recommend that the annual messages of the President be recast to provide a better basis for subsequent program evaluation. In particular, the Budget document should provide more of the elements of an annually revised resource allocation plan, as well as financial controls. It should review past performance against past objectives, give greater emphasis to stating the specific achievements expected from the major programs supported by the budget submission, and relate major current objectives to a long-range plan leading toward policy goals.

Although the President's Budget document, suitably revamped, could greatly strengthen program evaluation, it can deal only with the highlights of particularly significant programs. After the Budget is presented, each agency head should issue a statement to amplify those portions of the resource allocation plan for which he is responsible. This would ensure deeper coverage than is now possible in the Budget.

THE ROLE
OF THE EXECUTIVE BRANCH

In theory the Executive Branch is a hierarchy headed by the President, but in fact the relations between Cabinet officers and the President are more complex than those between division managers and the chief executive of a large business corporation. The first Budget Director, Charles G. Dawes, is said to have instructed one of his successors that Cabinet members were "vice presidents in charge of spending, and as such, the natural enemies of the President."

It is by no means clear, however, that department or agency heads are serving the President badly when they act as advocates for their particular programs. For they are expected not only to manage their resources efficiently but also to deal with special constituencies and with the career executives under them. Career executives are properly concerned with the institutional health of their organizations, and, more often than not, are motivated by a genuine conviction of the overriding importance of their programs to the nation. Their effectiveness depends on maintaining the support of the relevant Congressional subcommittees, as well as competing effectively for support within the Executive Branch.

Even the President must function both as manager of the federal government in the general interest and as a political leader of a party that consists of a coalition of groups with divergent interests. In view of the conflicting pressures facing top officials of the Executive Branch, it is not surprising when concern over the effective allocation and management of resources is submerged by the need to defend particular programs, arbitrate among jealous bureau chiefs, appease the Congress, or respond to special interests.

Strengthening Incentives
for Effective Management

Past efforts to improve the planning and management of federal programs have been impaired by a failure to come to grips with the incentives that guide the actions of those within the government establishment. The gap between the aspirations that motivated the Planning-Programming-Budgeting System and its actual achievements was in large part a result of failure to deal realistically with the existing incentives of government officials.

28.

Some current thought on public policy seems to suggest that the existing network of incentives be accepted entirely as it is, that the results of the interaction of existing incentives are as good as we can hope for, and that it is useless and perhaps pernicious to try to change incentives. While we are under no illusions about the complexity of the problem or the difficulty of restructuring incentives, we reject the position that it is hopeless or harmful to attempt to do so.

To strengthen the incentives for effective and responsive program management, it is necessary to increase the accountability of program managers to policy makers and of policy makers to the legislature and the public. Accountability for the substantive results of programs depends on two factors: (1) pinpointing of accountability for program results, supported by authority over program execution; and (2) the existence of an effective program execution and evaluation process.

The designation of managers responsible for program results is a key step in achieving program objectives. It must include the assignment of necessary authority over the use of resources and the direction of program activities in producing the specified results. Program evaluation can help to clarify the intent and objectives of high-level policy and thus serve as a guide to better program execution. To yield these benefits, agency heads and line program managers must be heavily involved in the evaluation process, and they must understand that the future of their agencies, programs, and careers will be affected by how well the process is handled. The cooperation of line program managers in the evaluation process depends on an understanding that it is an integral part of their management responsibility, and that it is one of the criteria for judging their performance.

But a commitment to program evaluation that begins and ends within the Executive Branch is likely to avoid some of the hardest issues, and even a Presidential commitment is likely to be eroded over time. To increase the incentives for improved program evaluation, the commitment should extend to publishing the result of such evaluation for use by the Congress and the public as well as by the Executive Branch. This is especially necessary in the evaluation of activities supported by grants-in-aid to state and local governments. The periodic review of legislative authorizations, recommended in the CED policy statement on *Making Congress More Effective*, would offer an ideal opportunity for Executive Branch and Congressional evaluation of programs.[1]

---

[1]/*Making Congress More Effective*, A Statement on National Policy by the Research and Policy Committee, CED (New York: September 1970), pp. 32-34.

What is needed is to achieve for program analysis and evaluation a status similar to that of data on national product, changes in the price level, and unemployment. Those data often touch areas of great political sensitivity and their publication conflicts with the interest of many, both within and outside government. Yet the commitment to develop them is sufficiently rooted in the federal establishment, the professional standards for judging them are sufficiently well-established, and—above all— the public expectation that they will be available is so strong that it would be impossible to tamper with or withhold them for political or administrative convenience. We believe that it is possible to achieve eventually a similar status for the results of program evaluation. The business community can play a useful role both in adding to the demand for published evaluations and in encouraging the establishment of professional standards for program analysis and evaluation.

Developing "Social Indicators"

Unless the government can acquire information for detecting and diagnosing social problems and for designing program solutions based on an understanding of cause-and-effect relationships, the public will become prisoner of what have been called "hidden policies." Examples are found in attempts to provide income support for dependent children, which undermine the family structure of a substantial and growing class of our population; in efforts to make home ownership more widespread, which increase *de facto* racial segregation in our cities; and in reclamation projects in California, which reduce the income of cotton farmers in Georgia and Texas and increase commodity support costs.

The Executive Branch has taken an important step toward exposing some of these hidden policies through its work on "social indicators" —measures of social conditions that reveal changes affecting the well-being of our society. Many of our most pressing social problems, such as environmental quality and medical care, involve matters that are either noneconomic and omitted entirely from the data by which we measure economic conditions and trends, or are imperfectly reflected in such data. In fact, our national income accounts include the market value of electricity produced with high sulfur coal, and the medical services required by an emphysema patient whose condition is aggravated by air pollution. Clearly, we need additional kinds of data to reflect the nature, dimensions, and costs of such conditions.

As a step in the development of social indicators, the Department of Health, Education, and Welfare mounted a program that led to the

30.

publication in 1969 of a document entitled *Toward A Social Report*. Subsequently, the National Goals Research Staff has been established in the Executive Office of the President, and the Office of Statistical Policy has undertaken efforts to develop statistical indicators of social conditions. However, these efforts have not evolved a framework for measuring social and environmental conditions comparable in scope and clarity to that with which we measure economic activity, imperfect though the latter may be, and it may well be impossible to devise one.

Nevertheless, better measures of social conditions have an important role to play. Although better measures of the conditions of our society will not always tell us directly where public action is needed or what form it should take, to say nothing of evaluating existing programs, such information is a necessary precondition for establishing consensus on priorities for public action. It can also be useful in suggesting to the private sector, including the management of business corporations, the forces at work in the environment, and desirable directions for the discharge of the social responsibilities of business.[2]

We recommend that the federal government sponsor continuing efforts to devise, improve, and publish measures of social and environmental conditions.

Another approach under development within the Executive Branch seeks to display in gross terms the impact of groups of government programs. These program overview summaries, like social indicators, are designed to provide a context for program evaluation rather than to compare and rank programs definitively. They display, for example, the geographic distribution of the outlays and benefits of various categories of federal programs (education, manpower development, health, etc.), and they also show for such categories the characteristics of the beneficiaries with respect to income, age, race, and urbanization.[3]

Program overviews, in conjunction with social indicators, can help provide a context for considering priorities and for directing the attention of government officials and the public toward policy issues requiring further analysis. When such issues are identified, more detailed analysis of the costs and effectiveness of alternative programs is required to contribute to the selection of specific programs. In order to implement these suggestions it may be necessary for the government to improve the scope and frequency of its data collection, particularly the census.

---

[2]/See *Social Responsibilities of Business Corporations,* A Statement on National Policy by the Research and Policy Committee, Committee for Economic Development (New York: June 1971), pp. 46-49.

[3]/See Appendix C.

Executive Reorganization

The establishment of many new programs with complex social objectives in the last decade has produced a situation in which most of the major purposes of the federal government involve the operations of several major agencies and more than one level of government. In the absence of effective procedures and incentives for coordination, such complexity invites confusion, ineffectiveness, and waste. For example, the educational deficiencies of the disadvantaged in our urban centers are believed to result from a combination of factors including poverty, family disruption, bad physical environment, and poor health, as well as inadequate schools.[4] Federal programs to deal with such an array of problems cross the organizational lines of many bureaus in the Department of Health, Education, and Welfare, the Department of Labor, the Department of Housing and Urban Development, and the Office of Economic Opportunity, and they cross similar organizational lines at local levels. Comparable illustrations could be drawn from many other problem areas, including urban transportation, manpower, and water pollution.

Programs that cross organizational boundaries tend to arise in problems that are changing rapidly. Typical of such problems are those stemming from the need to improve the status of minority groups, the increased urbanization and physical concentration of our society, and technological change. Governmental responsibilities cannot be discharged adequately for such problems within existing organizational frameworks of government agencies.

Reorganization of the Executive Branch is necessary from time to time to meet changing problems, but newly emerging problems cannot always be dealt with by reorganization. The operating requirements that brought agencies into existence often continue, while new problems are superimposed on them. To some extent, therefore, programs will always cut across the existing organizational structure, and government will always have to provide incentives for effective coordination of programs that do not fit the existing structure. When that structure comes under review, as it has in the present Administration, proposals for change must seriously consider what effect they will have on incentives to deal with problems comprehensively rather than piecemeal.

4/See *Education for the Urban Disadvantaged: From Preschool to Employment,* A Statement on National Policy by the Research and Policy Committee, Committee for Economic Development (New York: March 1971).

32.

Objectives of the reorganization proposed by the Administration include:

- *Linking programs with similar objectives under the management control of a single department.*

- *Providing departments with a comprehensive, national purpose in order to strengthen the ability of the government to serve the broad public interest and increase its accountability.*

- *Providing strong, department-wide policy and management machinery and a small number of administrative units for greater coordination in policy-setting and execution.*

- *Providing decision-making on grant-in-aid programs to states and local communities that occurs in the field, rather than in Washington.*[5]

If achieved, these objectives would increase accountability for results and would thereby increase the incentives for effective management; they would improve executive performance and increase the ability of the government to attract, retain, and motivate better executives; and they would make possible the introduction of constructive intra-departmental competition in place of the often wasteful competition among separate departments. Success in achieving the objectives and realizing their benefits will depend strongly on cooperation between the Executive Branch and the Congress in developing the specific plans for reorganization and on the adoption by each Branch of procedures and organization consistent with those of the other.[6] **We support the objectives of the President's reorganization plans and urge cooperation between the Executive Branch and the Congress in working out the details of an improved structure for the Executive Departments.**

THE ROLE OF CONGRESS

The Congress can play an essential role in making federal programs more responsive to the will of the people and in providing incentives for the Executive Branch to improve the process of resource allo-

---

[5]/For a discussion of the "Scope and Benefits of the Reorganization" in the proposed Department of Human Resources, see U.S. Office of Management and Budget, *Papers Relating to President's Departmental Reorganization Program: A Reference Compilation* (Washington, D.C.: U.S. Government Printing Office, 1971), pp. 107-110.

[6]/See *Making Congress More Effective,* A Statement on National Policy by the Research and Policy Committee, Committee for Economic Development (New York: September 1970), pp. 42-44.

cation and management. In particular, the Congress has the opportunity to bring pressure to bear for the development of stronger and more regular evaluation of programs in terms of their objectives. This Committee's recently issued statement, *Making Congress More Effective,* contains a number of recommendations relevant to the role of Congress in improving the effectiveness of federal programs. In summary we recommended that:

● **Means for comprehensive review of the annual budget be established and used, relating total revenues and expenditures to the state of the economy.**

● **Annual authorizations be discontinued; instead, authorizations should be made along program and project lines, fully funded, for minimum terms of four years.**

● **Evaluation of program performance, in terms of objectives as well as dollars, be heavily stressed.**

● **The federal fiscal year be changed to coincide with the calendar year, so that appropriations may always precede expenditures.**

● **Congress establish and observe deadline dates for both authorizations and appropriations.**

● **Better informational and analytical resources be provided for committees of Congress.**

Since the publication of that statement, the Legislative Reorganization Act of 1970 has become law. Its provisions will accomplish a number of the objectives of Congressional reform set forth by this Committee. The measures of particular concern to the present statement provide for comprehensive hearings on the budget prior to action on specific legislation and appropriations; require the President to supply five-year funding projections for any new or expanded programs and for legally committed or mandated programs; require legislative committees to accompany reported bills with five-year funding projections; strengthen the staff support available from the General Accounting Office, with emphasis on cost-benefit analysis and from the Congressional Research Service (formerly known as the Legislative Reference Service), and direct cooperation between the Comptroller General and the Executive Branch in the establishment of standard classifications for programs and activities of the federal government. **We applaud the re-**

34.

forms embodied in the Legislative Reorganization Act of 1970 and urge that they be put into effect promptly and vigorously. **We further recommend that an appropriate continuing committee of the Congress be assigned responsibility for monitoring and reporting periodically to the public on how the provisions of the Act are being carried out.**

The Congress can play an important role in strengthening program evaluation, including the analysis of alternative proposals, by incorporating into new authorizing legislation a requirement—and the necessary funds—for program evaluation. Such a requirement would bolster the ability of the Congress to discharge its responsibility for oversight of the Executive Branch, and would be particularly important in grant-in-aid programs, where the cost of providing for evaluation would otherwise have to be borne by state and local governments. Without such provision and support it is extremely unlikely that significant evaluation of such programs will take place. This requirement would be entirely in keeping with the Legislative Reorganization Act of 1970 and the Intergovernmental Cooperation Act of 1968.

We recommend that, in authorizing legislation, Congress adopt the practice of requiring periodic program evaluation and that it authorize funds for this purpose. This is particularly important for grant-in-aid programs, where federal support of evaluation at the state and local level may be the principal means of achieving any evaluation for a rapidly growing class of federal expenditures.

3 Developing Programs To Achieve Objectives

A program can be no better than the best of the alternative approaches considered. Too often the choice is between a little more and a little less of existing activities. Only rarely will operating units suggest cutting back drastically current activities, eliminating them, or replacing them with radically different alternatives that could achieve their objectives more efficiently. In developing and selecting government programs that will make the greatest contribution to national goals and objectives, three major improvements should be made: (1) the range of alternatives should be expanded; (2) experimental programs should be better planned and more widely used; and (3) program analysis should be strengthened.

EXPANDING THE RANGE OF ALTERNATIVES

Broadening the range of alternatives is especially important when new policy goals are identified, when priorities among goals change, or when evaluation of performance reveals that existing activities are not working properly.

Involving Operational Levels

In order to develop alternatives that are both practical and un-biased, there must be interaction between top policy-making and operational levels. Policy guidelines in the form of statements of goals and general resource limitations within each major category of programs should be provided from above. Operating units should respond by proposing alternative sets of objectives and programs for proceeding toward policy goals within the resource limitations. Alternatives should be reviewed at the policy level to ensure that all important options have been included; and, if alternatives are added, comments on them should be sought from the operating level.

One of the objectives in creating the Domestic Council in the 1970 reorganization of the Executive Office of the President was to strengthen the involvement of the Executive Office in the formulation of alternatives as a basis for program development. This restructuring of the process should also increase the involvement of the President in developing alternatives, which could help make program development more responsive to Presidential policies. Analogous arrangements involving agency heads more actively in the formulation of program alternatives within their agencies should also be sought. Small program analysis staffs responsive to the agency heads can assist in this function.

We recommend that policy-making officials of the federal government, with Presidential leadership, take an active role in developing and widening the range of program alternatives considered in the course of the resource allocation process. They should have staff support for this purpose. Operating levels should also be closely involved in the process, in response to guidelines on objectives and general resource limitations.

Alternatives to Federal Programs

To ensure that all important alternatives are considered, program development and evaluation should usually consider alternatives to government spending or direct federal operation of programs. This is especially important when issues involve "spillover" effects, which occur when neither the market nor any other social mechanism provides incentives for individuals to take into account the effects of their actions on others. For example, the control of water pollution can be sought by public expenditures on facilities to deal with wastes after they are in the watershed or by the imposition of effluent or user charges on polluters as a means of shifting the social costs of pollution to the activities that cause it. Another similar alternative to government spending would be a tax on the commodities that produce pollution; this would reduce the demand for such commodities.* In the event that effluent charges are infeasible or undesirable in a particular case, incentives can be changed by regulations that flatly prohibit excessive pollution.

---

*See Memorandum by MR. RICHARD C. GERSTENBERG, page 64.

The appropriate combination of these approaches depends on particular considerations of efficiency and equity. But it is important that the case for efficiency be given a hearing by the inclusion of alternatives such as user charges. Otherwise, there is no basis for estimating whether undue weight is being given to special interests at the expense of the general interest.

We recommend that analysis of programs involving government spending consider, where appropriate, alternatives that promote social ends by changing private incentives through user charges, taxes, or regulation of private activities. Where objectives can be achieved with equal effectiveness by providing incentives or market mechanisms such as user charges, or by regulation of the private sector, such a course should be preferred to additional public spending.

When the spillover effect takes the form of social benefits rather than costs, a subsidy may be an alternative to a direct program. A common form of subsidy is the tax relief incentive that exempts from taxation certain types of income or expenditures held to be socially desirable. These currently include interest and property tax deductions from personal income taxes, which have the primary effect of encouraging home ownership; such deductions provided an estimated $5.6 billion of tax relief in the fiscal year 1971. They also include the now defunct investment tax credit to stimulate spending by business firms on plant and equipment. Other forms of subsidy with similar characteristics are credit guarantees and interest subsidies.

Subsidies are often politically attractive since they benefit those directly affected, while their costs are diffused among all taxpayers. Tax relief incentives or credit guarantees, whose costs are not explicit and do not appear in the budget, are even more politically attractive than direct subsidies. Consequently, while they, like other subsidies, can be useful, they are likely to be even less vulnerable to scrutiny and criticism. This political advantage sometimes promotes their use in cases where economic efficiency calls for a tax, rather than a subsidy, and even in cases where they represent relatively inefficient types of subsidies.

When tax relief incentives, loan guarantees, or other indirect subsidies are used, their costs, including foregone tax revenues, should be estimated and published both at the inception of the program and on a continuing basis thereafter.

Direct federal spending does not mean that the federal government must be the immediate producer of the goods and services needed to achieve social objectives. The alternative approaches considered

38.

should include contracts with private individuals or groups, since such arrangements will bring into play the incentives for effectiveness and efficiency of profit and loss. A recently issued CED policy statement on the social responsibilities of business recommends that corporations undertake such contracts in implementing their social commitments.[1]

We recommend that in the analysis of most domestic programs consideration be given to entire or partial reliance on the private sector or state and local governments as alternatives to federal operation of federally-financed programs.*

BETTER USE
OF PLANNED EXPERIMENTS

Program analysis and selection in many of the newer areas of federal involvement, and in activities entailing state and local operations, must often rely on weak and incomplete information. When new and complex social issues are involved, there is no substitute for experiment to determine what works.[2]

In the face of ignorance and uncertainty, the alternatives are deliberate experiment, unconscious experiment, or inaction. Deliberate program experiment can save time and resources, and ultimately either achieve its intended goal or permit the program to be discontinued. Unconscious experiment, often in the guise of a crash program to deal with a crisis, spends large resources on a set of measures deemed plausible, given existing information. Recognition of failure or inefficiency is made difficult by the commitment to a particular "solution." More often, after a substantial waste of resources, the result is despair over the feasibility of achieving an important objective. The program of aid to families with dependent children, cited earlier, is an unconscious experiment with unfortunate "hidden" results.

A deliberate experiment should be designed to gather information economically and to test the feasibility of alternative methods, not to develop an immediate universal solution to the problem. It should explore a variety of approaches, make comparisons, and permit inferences about the effectiveness of the various approaches tried. It should

---

[1]/*Social Responsibilities of Business Corporations,* A Statement on National Policy by the Research and Policy Committee, Committee for Economic Development (New York: June 1971).

[2]/The planned exploitation of the diversity of state and local operating programs can achieve some of the goals of experimental programs. (See page 59 of this Statement.)

*See Memorandum by MR. RICHARD C. GERSTENBERG, page 64.

39.

be based on a plan that specifies the questions to be answered, the milestones at which evaluation is to occur, and the actions contemplated on the basis of the findings. Without such a plan, an experiment can become merely an excuse to justify indefinite continuation of activities that yield neither information nor program benefits commensurate with their costs.

Many government programs have been labelled "experimental," and hundreds of millions of dollars have been spent on such programs. Too often, however, the experimental label has been used as a substitute for clarity about program goals. Nevertheless, some promising innovations have been made. One of the most sophisticated experiments has been a project supported by the Office of Economic Opportunity to isolate the effects of income maintenance programs on family behavior patterns and labor force participation.

We recommend that deliberately planned experimental programs be used more often by federal agencies to gather information as a basis for program design, planning, and evaluation. Experimental plans should always provide for definite milestones at which results are to be evaluated and subsequent actions determined.

To gather information economically, the scale of experiments should be restricted to the minimum size needed to acquire representative data and test operational feasibility. Otherwise, the possibility of control and the range of variation that can be explored are diminished, seriously impairing the utility of the experiment. Moreover, unless the program is small enough to preserve the distinction between an experimental and an operational program, political pressures for extension, like those experienced in the Model Cities Program, will preempt the activity and make the purposes of the experiment largely irrelevant.

A clear understanding of the nature of experimental programs and their goals should also be conveyed to the Congress and the General Accounting Office by program administrators in order to avoid Congressional pressure for unwarranted expansion and Congressional recrimination when some approaches are discarded after evaluation. Congressional involvement should be sought by specifying the experimental nature of the program in proposed authorizing legislation and by including funds for evaluation in such legislation.

In order to permit flexibility and diversity in experimentation, we urge that the scale of the experiment be no larger than that needed to provide the desired information and test operational feasibility. Funds for evaluation should be included in legislation authorizing experimental programs.

STRENGTHENING
PROGRAM ANALYSIS

To design effective programs or to choose the best among a set of alternatives, it is important to be able to predict the social, economic, or environmental consequences of public action. For example, knowledge of cause and effect relationships is necessary in order to choose efficient programs for preschool education of disadvantaged children[3] and also to form judgments about the proper allocation of resources among programs such as Head Start, programs to improve education for older disadvantaged children, and other antipoverty programs. It is not enough to know that a policy objective is important; effective public action requires the estimation of cost and effectiveness, and where possible, the evaluation of benefits. It also requires estimation of the administrative feasibility of programs, and the ability to design approaches that either accommodate existing incentive structures or deliberately change them.

The role of program analysis is to increase usable information on these questions. It may take many forms, from rigorous mathematical formulation to verbal clarification; from elaborate, computer-based simulation to pencil and paper calculations. Too often, program analysis has to rely on assumptions only distantly related to experience; where relevant data exist or can be obtained, program analysis can be greatly strengthened. Program analysis is therefore a principal "client" for experiments and for program evaluation.

Tests of Program Efficiency and Effectiveness

Both the private transactions of the marketplace and the public business of the government must deal with many complex and diverse interests. Both subject activities to tests for survival—the businessman must avoid losses to survive and the politician must obtain reelection to remain in office. But politicians are rarely identified with or judged at the polls by a single program, and elections consequently provide no clear indication of public reaction to specific programs. Unlike the market

---

[3]/For a statement of the importance of education in dealing with poverty and of preschooling in equalizing educational opportunity for the disadvantaged, see *Education for the Urban Disadvantaged: From Preschool to Employment,* A Statement on National Policy by the Research and Policy Committee, Committee for Economic Development (New York: March 1971).

process, the political process does not automatically provide program managers, elected officials, or the public with tests of a program's value or efficiency. The resource allocation process must overcome the lack of such tests and the resulting weakening of incentives to improve, restrict, or eliminate low-priority or inefficient programs. To provide such tests is a principal task for program analysis.

The earliest systematic approach to the development of criteria for the evaluation of federal government programs was cost-benefit analysis applied to proposals for public works programs. This type of analysis estimates both costs and benefits in dollar terms, and applies the ratio of the discounted present value of the future stream of benefits and costs to evaluate the programs. Approval of a program requires benefits at least equal to costs.

The benefits are an estimate of what consumers of the goods or services to be produced would be willing to pay for them if they were available for purchase. For example, the benefits of a flood control project might include the value of property saved, of irrigation water, and of the recreational opportunities afforded by the lakes created by the project. Therefore cost-benefit analysis is basically a market-oriented approach to the evaluation of government programs. In cases where government programs produce goods and services with a market value, cost-benefit analysis identifies those goods and services whose costs can be recovered by sale to individual consumers and therefore eliminates those that are analogous to losing business in the private sector.

We believe that cost-benefit analysis should be applied to those aspects of government programs whose output the market can value even if the decision has been made not to charge users, or whose output results in an increase in the efficiency of markets causing an increase in GNP. For example, cost-benefit analysis is an appropriate criterion of the efficiency of activities such as the provision of improved campsites in the national parks or the Atomic Energy Commission's uranium enrichment program to supply fuel for commercial energy production. But even here benefits that exceed costs mean simply that the activity can pay its way and not necessarily that it is best carried on by government rather than by private firms or quasi-governmental organizations.

We recommend that cost-benefit analysis, with benefits as well as costs expressed in dollars, be applied to those program outputs for which market values can be estimated.

The outcome of government programs depends on private as well as government decisions. Prediction of the effects of programs must be based on an understanding of the interaction between the two. Estimates of the economic benefits of programs to increase the supply of a commodity through government-sponsored research and development should take into account the fact that the price will be affected. Estimates of the results of highway building programs should take into account their effects on where people live and work. Subsidized flood plan insurance may induce people to live in high-risk areas. Subsidized waste treatment plants may result in pollution abatement approaches that are less efficient than internal plant controls.[4] Every federal program affects the incentives and behavior of large numbers of private individuals, firms, and governmental units, often in subtle and unexpected ways.

An understanding of individual decision processes and of the way they are affected by programs is essential for making valid estimates of program effects. But often such estimates are based on arbitrary assumptions. Program analysis should involve a more realistic appraisal of market behavior; and of the effect of a program on the incentives of private individuals, and those of state and local governments.

Public Goods and Cost-Effectiveness Analysis

Critics of the cost-benefit approach have contended that the market value of benefits is too narrow a concept for evaluating government programs. Some have proposed widening its applicability by adding to "primary" benefits an estimate of "secondary" benefits. Because no widely accepted definition of secondary benefits exists, their inclusion would increase the opportunities for special pleading on behalf of projects that are too inefficient to qualify otherwise. Nevertheless, we agree that the market value of the output of government programs is too narrow a concept for the full evaluation of most activities of government.

We are all familiar with private goods and services which we buy and consume. Among these are some produced by the government, such as the publications of the Government Printing Office. But most important government programs are supposed to make available goods or services that cannot be sold. The purest example of these "public goods" is national security. Public goods can only be consumed in common. Nuclear war is deterred for all of us if it is deterred at all. Therefore, it

[4]/See Allen V. Kneese, "Environmental Pollution: Economics and Policy," *American Economic Review,* Vol. 61, No. 2 (May 1971), p. 163.

is impossible to exclude anyone from the enjoyment of the benefits of national security, whether or not he has paid for his share of it. Unlike a pair of shoes that will be used only by the person who pays for them, no one has an individual incentive to pay for national security, and the market mechanism cannot determine how much of it should be provided. The level of spending on national security and other public goods must therefore be decided collectively through the government.

Public goods are also found in domestic programs such as education. For a self-governing society wants to achieve minimum educational standards for all its people. But education also constitutes a private good. Individuals want and are willing to pay for education for themselves and their children to increase the quality of their lives and their earning power.

When we evaluate the benefits of a program to improve the education of disadvantaged children, the increase in their future productivity and earning power can be estimated in dollars, as can savings due to reductions in future requirements for social services. But these clearly do not exhaust the benefits of better education for disadvantaged children. If better education is associated with public goods like lower crime rates, more constructive participation in political and social life, and better family environments, program analysis should attempt to estimate these benefits as well. The public goods aspects of a program to improve education therefore have to be expressed in terms of social variables, as well as in dollar benefits.

This kind of analysis has been named "cost-effectiveness" analysis, since it measures programs in terms of dollar costs on one side of the equation and various degrees of effectiveness on the other.[5] Only limited conclusions can be reached by cost-effectiveness analysis. There is no objective basis for determining whether a program that leads to a one per cent decrease in the rate of violent crime and a two per cent reduction in the rate of family abandonment is to be preferred to one of equal cost that reverses the percentages.

More broadly, although cost-effectiveness analysis is appropriate for such programs as urban renewal and space exploration, it provides no basis for determining the best allocation of resources between them, or the proper level for either. Such priorities have to be developed by the political process with the benefit of whatever quantitative or qualitative information analysis can supply.

---

[5]/See Appendix D.

44.

However, cost-effectiveness analysis can help considerably in comparing alternative programs. For any given set of program benefits, it is possible to select the alternative that achieves them at least cost. And in comparing equal cost alternatives it can indicate how much of one benefit must be given up to increase another. Clarifying such "trade-offs" can often focus the judgments of policy makers on new combinations of activities that are superior to any of the original alternatives.

In cases where program objectives include public goods for which it is impossible to establish a market value, we recommend that cost-effectiveness analysis be applied to select the most efficient among a set of alternatives, to display tradeoffs among objectives at equal cost, and, where possible, to suggest new and more efficient alternatives.

Frequently, programs with partially noneconomic objectives, as in the case of education, will also have an economic aspect. In this case, cost effectiveness is the appropriate kind of analysis. Each dimension of program effectiveness should be indicated separately, including its excess of dollar benefits over cost, if any. Since the benefits of many programs are not measurable in dollar terms, it is arbitrary to translate these noneconomic effects into dollar terms and to include them as secondary benefits.

If a program's output of public goods, its redistribution of income, and its noneconomic benefits are all translated into dollar terms and added, the weights must necessarily be assigned arbitrarily by the analyst, since determination of the value of such program outputs is essentially a political matter. Moreover, a public works program, for example, may combine income distribution, stimulation of regional economies, and other nonmarket benefits into an over-all measure of secondary benefits, which would make it difficult or impossible to compare the program's effectiveness in achieving these ends with other alternatives, including direct transfers of income and general fiscal policy.

Construction of a dam that proves to be an inefficient water resources project may also be an inefficient way to increase the income of the poor and to stimulate economic activity in the area. Moreover, alleged secondary benefits to one group or region must be weighed against secondary costs to other groups or regions.

In short, so-called secondary benefits should be presented in terms of specific types of program accomplishment rather than in terms of an over-all dollar aggregate. They should be presented separately for each type of benefit, and they should be net of secondary costs to other groups or regions.

45.

Guidelines for
Estimating Costs and Benefits

The calculation of dollar costs and benefits, where appropriate, presents a number of specific problems. These include estimation of proper prices for government-provided goods and services that could be sold but are made available free of charge; proper treatment of the effect of the monopoly power of government with respect to many of the goods it actually does sell; and discounting procedures for programs that generate costs and outputs over a period of time. We believe that the use of dollar calculations should be based on the fact that the resources involved in government programs are being diverted from uses in the private sector. Calculations should therefore be carried out in a way that permits tests of the economic efficiency of government programs consistent with those applied to private resource-using activities.

Clarification and consistency have been particularly lacking in discounting future costs and benefits.[6] Procedures have been a crazy quilt of inconsistent and arbitrary approaches. In addition to problems in the method of application, a better basis is needed for determining the discount rates to be used. Although economists are not agreed on the appropriate value of the discount rate to be applied by government, the overwhelming professional opinion is that the rates actually used have been too low, and as a result the efficiency of long-lived construction projects and other capital-using activities has been overestimated. The Joint Economic Committee has done much in the recent past to focus attention on this issue and to clarify it.

In 1969 the Bureau of the Budget (now the Office of Management and Budget) took an important step toward rationalizing the situation by issuing guidelines for rates to be applied to discounting future costs and benefits. The guidelines established procedures for discounting costs and benefits and established the current yield on federal bonds of long maturity as a *minimum* rate to be applied, pending the results of a study to establish a methodology for determining the appropriate rate and for estimating how much higher than the minimum such a rate ought to be. These guidelines are an important step in the direction of eliminating the bias toward arbitrary displacement of private by public activities and dis-

---

6/The extent of the inconsistency was vividly shown by a survey conducted by the General Accounting Office. See U.S. General Accounting Office, *Survey of Use by Federal Agencies of the Discounting Technique in Evaluating Future Programs; Report to the Joint Economic Committee*, by the Comptroller General of the United States (Washington, D.C.: 1968).

46.

tortion of federal program design that has resulted from artificially low discount rates used in analyzing government programs.

We commend the General Accounting Office, Joint Economic Committee, and the Office of Management and Budget for their efforts to improve the estimation of future costs and benefits. **We recommend that the Office of Management and Budget periodically review the discount rate used in cost-benefit studies, and pending the determination of a methodology for estimating the appropriate rate, program costs and benefits should be estimated by using a range of rates with the minimum at least as high as the yield on long-term Treasury bonds.**

We note that the 1969 guidelines are limited to the evaluation of government programs and presumably are not intended to apply to the pricing of services produced by the government. We recognize that it will often be socially desirable to subsidize such goods and services. Nevertheless, in order to identify the subsidy clearly as a basis for making decisions about the activities, a subsidy-free price should be calculated to permit estimation of the amount of subsidy involved.

Government programs often use resources that are not reflected in the current budget of the agency using them. These include government-owned capital with other potential applications, notably government-owned land, and plant and equipment. They also include goods and services that are provided by one agency for use by another, such as nuclear warheads provided by the Atomic Energy Commission for the use of the Department of Defense. Finally, they include the present value of the cost of employee retirement benefits. The full cost of such resources, including current charges for capital assets used, should be a part of the costs that enter cost-effectiveness analysis.

We recommend that the Office of Management and Budget issue guidelines clarifying the pricing of goods and services provided by the government and the estimation of costs that enter cost-effectiveness analysis.

Correcting the Bias Toward Underestimation of Program Costs

Underestimation of the costs of government programs has become commonplace. Although the problem has received most public attention in relation to military procurement, it also exists in many domestic programs, especially in the newer programs with social objectives. The early years of the Medicare and Medicaid programs provide clear illus-

...us of the failure in government to estimate costs accurately. For ...mple, in the Budget for the fiscal year 1969, supplemental appropria-...ions to the fiscal year 1968 requests for both Medicare and Medicaid amounted to more than 40 per cent of the original requests. Both were attributed to a combination of unexpected price increases and higher-than-expected use of the programs.

Incorrect cost estimation usually has two distinct causes: (1) imprecision in specifying program content, and (2) analytic deficiencies or deliberate underestimation of program costs.

The first is a deficiency of program planning. Its remedies lie in improving the specification of alternatives and in increasing the understanding of the substantive activities to be undertaken. Often this deficiency is a result of an inadequate assessment of the impact of a program on private decisions. For example, the unanticipated increases in the cost of medical care and in the demand for the benefits of the Medicare and Medicaid programs represent a failure to evaluate the impact of a federal program on activities previously rationed by the market.

However, when programs are undertaken in government for the first time, there is bound to be a great deal of uncertainty about their content and hence about their costs. Uncertainty about program content is difficult or impossible to eliminate in many research and development projects and in many new areas of social activity. In such cases, allowance for uncertainty should be explicitly included in the program planning process. The possible effects on costs should be shown by displaying "possible high" as well as "expected" estimates, which would permit policy makers to judge whether the program is desirable in the face of the uncertainties.

We recommend that cost estimates reflect program uncertainty by showing "possible high" as well as "expected" estimates in program analysis that is prepared for use in the resource allocation and program planning process.

The second major class of error results from combinations of analytic deficiencies and from too much dependence on estimates prepared by those with a vested interest in making the proposed program look attractive. "Bidding in" with low-cost estimates by agencies anxious to fund a program or by contractors anxious to sell equipment produces a pervasive bias toward underestimation of cost in many programs. Control of this bias requires independent checks on estimates and penalties for organizations and individuals involved in biased cost estimation. Such penalties should be reflected in procedures for evaluating agency management within the government, and in contract terms that penalize cost overruns by contractors. When the scale of program activities is controllable, cost overruns due to biased estimation should not be allowed to result in an increase in total spending for the program; program activities should be scaled down at least in proportion to the overrun.

We recommend that more sources of independent cost estimates be developed at policy-making levels, and used to reduce biases toward underestimation of program costs in the resource allocation and program planning process. Unjustifiable cost overruns should be penalized through administrative action and contract terms.

4 Program Execution and Performance Evaluation

After policy decisions have established program goals and objectives and the planning process has developed the means to achieve them, there must be effective execution of the decisions and monitoring of performance to determine whether policy and plans are being carried out effectively. The budget translates program decisions into a specific allocation of resources and thus provides a link between policy and plans on one hand and execution on the other. It is the task of evaluation to bring actual program experience to bear on major reviews of policy issues, and to determine whether existing programs are achieving their objectives. In this way evaluation can serve as a basis for future planning and management decisions.

PROGRAM BUDGETING

Recommendations to improve decision making in the federal government have usually included revisions of the classification of activities used in budgeting and appropriations. The two most widely-known efforts were those of the Hoover Commission in 1949, and the Planning-Programming-Budgeting System introduced in 1965. Both of these endeavors to introduce *program* budgeting were part of a wider set of recommendations aimed at improving management in the federal government, and both included attempts, in the words of the Hoover Commission, to center attention "... on the function or activity—on the accomplishment of the purpose—instead of on lists of employees or authorizations of purchases."[1]

Program budgeting has four principal goals. (1) It seeks to introduce classification systems (called "program structures") that categorize activities by the type of objectives to be accomplished (outputs) rather

---

[1]/U. S. Commission on Organization of the Executive Branch of the Government, *The Hoover Commission Report on Organization of the Executive Branch of the Government* (New York: McGraw-Hill, 1949), p. 36.

than the type of goods and services that constitute the immediate objects of agency expenditure (inputs). (2) It attempts to array under each program category or subcategory *all* the costs of the entire system of activities associated with a particular output, regardless of organizational structure. (3) It tries to orient the program manager not only to the allocation of resources but to the specific results he is expected to accomplish with them. (4) It seeks to provide the basis for budgetary, accounting, and reporting control.

All four goals are valuable in presenting a picture of how resources have been allocated among the various purposes of government, and in determining the cost of each kind of output produced. **We support the objectives of program budgeting and recommend that the federal government continue its development.**[2]

Nevertheless, we believe that arguments over the virtues and limitations of an objectives-oriented classification system for program activities have been overstated and have unduly detracted from efforts to improve the over-all process of resource allocation, program development, program execution, and program evaluation. A better budget format is merely one of a number of needed changes, and the complexity of program objectives means that there is no uniquely suitable program structure.

An appropriately designed program structure can show the implications of a given set of program choices for specific program costs and outputs. But no format can itself point the way to program choice, nor can it provide adequately all the information needed to evaluate program performance. At best a standard format can give a very crude approximation of costs associated with a complex program. It can also offer a small number of standard, numerical output measures that may be illuminating but would not give an adequate indication of program performance for evaluation purposes. Program choice and program evaluation should be based on detailed and flexible measures of costs and output.

The issue of program budgeting is not whether to choose a traditional budget format or a program budget format. Congressional preferences, based on committee jurisdictions and familiarity with the existing format, have prevented abandonment of the traditional budget. But, Congressional opposition apart, complete abandonment of organizational categories in the budget format would present serious problems.

---

[2]/See *Control of Federal Government Expenditures,* A Statement on National Policy by the Research and Policy Committee, Committee for Economic Development (New York: January 1955), pp. 11-13.

When a system of activities constituting a program cuts across organizational lines, it is impossible to satisfy all management information needs with a single standard classification structure.

An organizational format will not display the implications of program choices or provide a bench mark for program evaluation. A program budget format will not show the impact of a set of program choices on the resources or work loads of the operating units responsible for program execution. Without adequate presentations of both types and a clear way of relating the two, choices made in program terms cannot be related to organizational assignments for program execution. An appropriate system should be based on common data elements that can be aggregated on either organizational or program lines.

The federal government's efforts to introduce program budgeting have not yet extended to the development of a government-wide program structure. Lack of consistency among program structures makes it impossible to measure the extent of agency overlaps. Until it is possible to aggregate the overlapping activities of different agencies, the program budget will fail to display the total of resources allocated to the achievement of different objectives.

Presently, there are three principal budget classification systems: the first based on organization and appropriations; a second that categorizes government activities by functions such as national defense, space research and technology, agriculture and rural development; and a third that categorizes them by the program structures introduced by the Planning-Programming-Budgeting System.[3] The first two systems are government-wide systems; the program structures are not. We doubt that a useful purpose is served by proliferating budget classification systems. Rather, we believe that the functional categories and program structures should be merged into a single government-wide system that is suitable for displaying the consequences of program choices.

The Legislative Reorganization Act of 1970 requires that the Secretary of the Treasury and the Director of the Office of Management and Budget, in cooperation with the Comptroller General, establish standard program and activity classifications. **We recommend a consolidation of the existing functional and program budget classification systems into a single, government-wide system suitable for displaying program costs and outputs, and that the resulting system be based on data elements that permit aggregation on organization, appropriation, or program lines.** Such a consolidation would retain one basic classifica-

---

[3]/See Appendix E.

tion by organization and appropriation and another by program; to-gether they should provide the basic framework for presentation of the budget. Of course, in addition to matters of format, program budgeting reflects an emphasis on performance, which is the important ingredient in the concept.

MULTI-YEAR PLANNING

Program decisions usually have cost and output implications that go well beyond the budget year. When programs involve substantial capital investment, expenditures may precede output by several years. Full funding of capital investment projects is desirable for bringing commitments of future outlays into focus for individual programs. In addition, capital outlays may, in effect, commit the government to oper-ating outlays over a long period of time. Even if programs do not involve large outlays of physical capital, new programs invariably have a build-up period in which staff is being assembled and trained, so that relatively small current costs have to be regarded as the seeds of larger future costs and output. Demonstration and experimental programs are special cases of this kind of growth; they are undertaken in the expectation that suc-cess will result in larger outlays.

Perhaps the most important kind of commitment of future re-sources outside of specific statutory or contractual commitments is that which arises out of major goals publicly adopted by the President. Such goals are usually focused on accomplishments years in the future, and are often intended to commit the country to a course of action which must transcend short-run pressures in order to succeed. If the govern-ment is to avoid overcommitment of resources and to establish a frame-work for judging programs with long-range costs and outputs, it must have not only a comprehensive plan for the budget year but also one that goes several years into the future. The appropriate period for multi-year planning varies among programs, but five years appears to be a reason-able period for evaluating the over-all commitment of future resources by the government.

The federal Budget for 1971 and the 1971 Economic Report of the President included for the first time projections of government rev-enues and expenditures five years into the future (see Figure 4). The projections showed the difference between future revenues and expendi-ture commitments as "funds to cover new initiatives" including possible tax reductions or budget surpluses.

53.

The Legislative Reorganization Act of 1970 requires the projection five years into the future of summaries of estimated expenditures required under continuing programs with legal commitments or mandated under existing law; in addition, five-year funding estimates are required to accompany requests for authorization to expand programs or to establish new programs. This requirement and the projections shown in the 1971 and 1972 Budget documents are both useful steps toward the establishment of a multi-year planning framework for federal programs. We believe these requirements should be broadened. **We recommend that the Budget document present a five-year projection by major program categories showing program expenditures for each year implied by the commitments inherent in existing program strategy. Major anticipated program achievements should also be shown over the five-year period as a bench mark for evaluating program performance.**

Figure 4: PROJECTED RESOURCES

(Fiscal years. In billions of current dollars.)

Item	1971 estimated	1975 projected
Revenues	$202	$266
Outlays:		
Current programs	200	228
Price, pay, and workload increases		(20)
Net increase in other current programs		(8)
Initiatives reflected in this budget	3	18
Less: Outlays for terminations, restructuring,		
and reductions	—2	—2
Total	201	244
Funds to cover new initiatives		22

Source: U.S. Bureau of the Budget, The Budget of the United States Government, Fiscal Year 1971, *p. 59.*

In emphasizing the need for improvements in long-range planning, we do not intend to minimize the need for communicating short-term attainable objectives to responsible program managers as a basis for their activities. This is especially important in light of changes that occur in the budget process. Short-term objectives must be adjusted to reflect realistic expectations of what can be achieved within the limits of the authorized funding. The failure to lay out a short-term work plan is often the reason why federal programs do not function effectively.

PERFORMANCE EVALUATION

Without procedures for observing and analyzing the actual performance of programs, the federal government is like a navigator who relies entirely on dead reckoning for a long voyage. Yet a recent study of social programs by the Urban Institute has concluded "that substantial work in this field has been almost nonexistent...Many small studies around the country have been carried out with such lack of uniformity of design and objective that the results rarely are comparable or responsive to the questions facing policy makers."[4]

The General Accounting Office, in reviewing the performance of economic opportunity programs as directed by the 1967 amendments to the Economic Opportunity Act of 1964, summarized the major requirements for adequate evaluation of those programs as follows:

> *There must be a comprehensive evaluation plan.*
> *Evaluation must extend to research and demonstration projects.*
> *Evaluation should extend to alternative programs.*
> *There must be an adequate evaluation staff.*
> *Continuing research must be carried on.*
> *Reliable and pertinent data must be available.*[5]

Observation and analysis of actual program performance are necessary to support major reviews of policy, to determine the validity of the planning and budgeting process in translating policy goals into operational plans and objectives, and to assess management performance

[4]/Joseph S. Wholey and others, *Federal Evaluation Policy: Analyzing the Effects of Public Programs* (Washington, D.C.: Urban Institute, 1970), p. 15.

[5]/U.S. General Accounting Office, *Review of Economic Opportunity Programs; Report to the Congress,* by the Comptroller General of the United States (Washington, D.C.: 1969), pp. 173-174.

in the achievement of stated program objectives. To perform these functions, two distinct but complementary approaches are required: (1) evaluation to support policy review, which requires intensive, special purpose analysis of program performance; and (2) evaluation to determine whether stated program objectives are being achieved, which relies on regular monitoring of operations by program managers.

Evaluation for Policy Review

To support major policy decisions affecting the initiation of new programs, the reorientation of existing programs, or the termination of those that have outlived their usefulness, it is valuable and often essential to have observation and analysis of the effectiveness of existing programs ("impact" is the term often used in regard to social programs). Such observations should measure not only the achievement of stated program objectives but also unanticipated side effects—including effects on other programs—and problems. Often such measurements must also be compared with a control group outside the program. For these reasons, and because of the possibility of institutional bias, evaluations of program impact cannot rely exclusively on normal lines of program management but require the involvement of policy-making officials and the Congress, adequately supported by program evaluation staffs. Intensive evaluations of effectiveness cannot be performed for each program every year without imposing unreasonable staff requirements; they should take place when a major policy issue arises, or when a renewal of program authorization is required.

A recent survey of resources for evaluation in selected social programs indicates that the resources spent on program evaluation have not exceeded one-half of one per cent of program funding, even if allowance is made for the cost of in-house staff[6] (see Figure 5). The authors concluded that evaluation in the Office of Education and in manpower programs, neither of which exceeded one tenth of one per cent, were "grossly underfunded." This is particularly significant in view of the great need for evaluation in the new social areas of federal action. Still, these selected programs have probably received more evaluation than the average program.

The General Accounting Office, in its review of economic opportunity programs, has presented an estimate of the cost of evaluation in

---

6/Joseph S. Wholey and others, *Federal Evaluation Policy*, p. 78.

Figure 5: RESOURCES FOR EVALUATION IN SELECTED SOCIAL PROGRAMS

Department	1969 Program Funding ($ Millions)	1969 Federal Grants and Contracts for Evaluation ($ Millions)	Evaluation Effort as Per Cent of Program Funding (%)	In-House Professional Staff
Total (of Selected Programs)	**3,877**	**17.0**	**0.4**	**76**
Department of Labor (Selected Programs)	**1,010**	**4.1**	**0.4**	**28**
Manpower Development and Training Programs	240	0.3	0.1	28
Programs Funded Under Economic Opportunity Act	665	2.8	0.4	
Work Incentive Program	105	1.0	1.0	
Department of Health, Education, and Welfare (Selected Programs)	**1,610**	**4.0**	**0.3**	**26**
Maternal and Child Health Programs	210	1.4	0.7	13
Vocational Education	250	0.1	0.03	1
Title I, Elementary and Secondary Education Act	1120	0.6	0.05	9
Follow Through	30	1.9	6.3	3
Office of Economic Opportunity (Selected Programs)	**1,003**	**6.5**	**0.7**	**14**
Community Action Program (Local initiative programs only)	331	2.2	0.7	7
Head Start	330	2.4	0.7	2
Job Corps	295	1.9	0.6	4
Legal Services Program	47	0	0	1
Department of Housing and Urban Development (Selected Programs)	**254**	**2.4**	**0.9**	**8**
Model Cities	254	2.4	0.9	8

Note: The funding for evaluation grants and contracts excludes cost for in-house staff, administrative costs for monitoring activities, and some costs for data collection.
Source: Data from Joseph S. Wholey and others, Federal Evaluation Policy, p. 79.

57.

the Office of Economic Opportunity. Over the period 1964-1967, this cost was estimated at $22 million, with 60 per cent spent on evaluation work by contractors.[7] During this period, the Office of Economic Opportunity spent nearly $5 billion on innovative programs to achieve objectives where there was little or no previous experience as a guide. And the Office of Economic Opportunity is widely acknowledged to be among the best of the federal agencies with respect to evaluation.

More recently, evaluation has been receiving greater emphasis and increased resources as a result of heightened interest in both the Executive Branch and the Congress. The 1967 amendments to the Economic Opportunity Act, which authorized and directed increased evaluation efforts by the Office of Economic Opportunity, and also directed the independent evaluation by the Comptroller General referred to above, were important breakthroughs in Congressional emphasis on evaluation. In 1967 and 1968, eleven pieces of legislation authorized sums for appropriation to the Secretary of Health, Education, and Welfare for evaluation in amounts ranging from one-half of one per cent to such sums as the Appropriations Committees deemed necessary. **We urge that Congress continue and accelerate its recent trend toward explicit authorization and direction of evaluation efforts by the Executive Branch in legislation authorizing programs, and that it use the strengthened staff resources provided by the Legislative Reorganization Act of 1970 to obtain more independent evaluation.**

Setting aside funds for evaluation is particularly important for the large and growing portion of federal expenditures that go to support programs operated by state and local governments. Congress has deliberately restricted federal control or involvement in many such programs; the current trend toward greater local discretion in the use of federal money through bloc grants (and perhaps by revenue sharing in the future) is likely to reduce federal involvement even further. We believe that the federal government has an obligation to strengthen program evaluation where federal funds are being spent, whether or not the federal government takes part in or is the primary recipient of the results. **We recommend that Congress authorize funds for evaluating grant-in-aid programs even in cases where the federal government will not take part in the evaluation directly; in such cases, it should stipulate that the evaluations be made publicly available by the state or local units conducting them.**

7/U.S. General Accounting Office, *Review of Economic Opportunity Programs*, p. 173.

58.

Grant-in-aid programs provide an opportunity as well as a problem for program evaluation. Their natural diversity provides a built-in form of experimental variation that can supplement the controlled experiments discussed earlier. This is fortunate. Although controlled experiments should be used more frequently, they are too expensive and too politically charged to satisfy entirely the requirements for performance data. But the diversity of state and local operations can be exploited only if there is a comprehensive plan for data gathering designed to provide the information on cause and effect in social problems and government programs that is required by the policy process.

In order to achieve effective evaluation, it may be necessary to provide for the accumulation of special information not needed—and therefore not kept—in normal administrative practice; to gather information by special questionnaires or performance tests; to establish control groups; and above all, to follow specific population samples long enough to establish such long-term program effects as the effect of job training on employability and earnings.

The actual data gathering is best carried out under the responsibility of the program manager and during the course of program operations. This avoids the need of a large organization for evaluation which parallels the line operating organization. Nevertheless, evaluation plans must be developed through the coordinating efforts of policy level officials in the agencies and in the Office of Management and Budget. **We recommend that the office of the agency head and the Office of Management and Budget take active roles in designing and coordinating program evaluation plans. We further recommend that they review such plans, their costs, and the performance of program managers in carrying them out as part of the normal program review.**

Evaluating the Achievement of Stated Program Objectives

We have already noted the importance of evaluating program performance against the objectives which justified the initiation or funding of the program. Clarity in operational objectives is recognized as basic for guiding and evaluating program management, and for testing the validity of the planning process. Yet in the federal government current practice on this score is far from satisfactory.

> . . . *The most clear-cut evidence of the primitive state of federal self-evaluation lies in the widespread failure of agencies even to*

59.

spell out program objectives . . . there is no standard against which to measure whether the direction of a program or its rate of progress is satisfactory.[8]

Line managers are explicitly responsible for resource consumption but not always for results . . . Lacking clearly stated goals and objectives against which to measure . . . program performance, agency performance measurement systems have been relatively ineffective.[9]

Failure to achieve stated program objectives may not always reflect unfavorably on the usefulness of the program. But such failure imposes substantial requirements for information about the conduct of the program, and raises questions about the assumptions made in planning for it. Is the problem unrealistic program planning, inefficient execution, or is it an unforeseeable contingency not likely to occur again? If the difficulty lies in the planning, it may be necessary to reevaluate the decision to undertake the program. Even if the benefits of a program are still deemed to be important, higher costs than anticipated may suggest that a program be cut back or cancelled. A program that provides job training for hard-core unemployed, for example, may be worth doing at its planned cost per person productively employed but not at twice this cost. At the higher cost, other alternatives for dealing with the problem may be preferred.

The development of measures of program output is crucial to the utility of program evaluation. Oversimplification of output measurement can result in discrediting the entire evaluation process. Even worse, inappropriate output measures can give program managers incentives that run counter to the actual program objectives. An effective evaluation system should establish measures-of-output "rules" under which program managers should try to "score" as high as they can.

For example, evaluation of a manpower training program by the number of cases handled without adequate supporting data may motivate the program manager to maximize the case flow by superficial treatment. Even if there is follow-up investigation of the subsequent employment records, the program manager may be motivated to taking the easiest cases rather than dealing with the hard-core unemployed.

---

[8]/Joseph S. Wholey and others, *Federal Evaluation Policy*, p. 15.

[9]/McKinsey and Company, Inc., *Strengthening Program Planning, Budgeting, and Management in the Federal Government* (Washington, D.C.: December 1970), p. 9. This report was submitted to the Office of Management and Budget.

60.

As we indicated earlier, no single element can provide an adequate indication of program effectiveness. Although a program manager in government is responsible for producing specified results with a specified level of resources, for most government activities no direct analogy to the "profit center" in private business is available for use as a device for simultaneously motivating management and measuring its performance.

Because government program activities are typically so complex, mistakes will inevitably be made in the choice of output measures. They are so critical an aspect of effectively decentralized management that a review of their effects is as important as a review of the substantive achievement of the program. Only by periodic review of the adequacy of output measures at policy levels in the Executive Branch and in the Congress can mistakes be corrected and an appropriate set of measures be developed.

We recommend that the program objectives and cost estimates on the basis of which a program was funded constitute the criteria for evaluating its performance. The objectives should be adopted only after careful consideration of the incentives they establish for program managers. The suitability of program objectives should be reviewed as an integral part of periodic program review by policy-level officials.

STAFFING FOR EVALUATION

For the planning and review of program evaluations, small staffs reporting to policy level officials are needed. The skills required are similar to those of the program analysis staffs discussed earlier; but the two functions should be separated, in order to avoid institutional bias in favor of programs proposed by the program analysis staff, and to avoid diverting the efforts of the program evaluation staff into program planning. They should, however, report to a common head below the level of the agency head.

Recruiting for program analysis and evaluation staffs is difficult. The combination of analytic and substantive skills required is still rare, though increasing. Although university graduate programs more and more are including the kind of interdisciplinary curricula required, faster progress would be desirable. The government's need for program analysts and evaluators should be taken into account by agencies such as the National Science Foundation in targeting programs to support graduate education.

As already noted, the primary burden of data gathering for program evaluation should fall on the line organization for program management. Some reliance on contractual services is useful, however, to supplement "in-house" efforts to provide continuing long-term research and to provide independence of views. Outside groups are useful particularly for intensive special purpose evaluation. In addition to analytic firms and nonprofit institutes, quasi-governmental organizations such as the National Academy of Sciences can be useful in assembling *ad hoc* evaluation groups—including persons drawn from the academic community—and in developing professional standards and accountability systems. The use of outside groups is particularly important in supplementing state and local program evaluation capabilities.

We recommend that small staffs be maintained to assist policy-making officials in program analysis and evaluation. The government should take a more active role in encouraging the kind of interdisciplinary graduate curricula required for training such staffs. "In-house" staffs should be supplemented by the use of contractual arrangements with outside groups; the government should foster through quasi-governmental organizations the development of professional standards and accountability for such groups.

Memoranda of Comment, Reservation, or Dissent

Page 9—By JOHN D. HARPER, with which ALLAN SPROUL has asked to be associated:

It is difficult to criticize this policy statement, in view of the fact that it seems to advocate the normal management procedures that would come from the Harvard Business School or any other modern management group. I do have very serious reservations as to the value of the report. While it is a "motherhood statement," with which few can argue, it may be useful in helping to establish criteria and promote public discussion. However, it may give the CED and its members an unjustified sense of accomplishment.

The report is insensitive to the political realities of Washington and I do not believe that there will be any constructive change as a result of this report. The Executive Branch under recent Presidents has continued to expand. This is particularly true of the White House function itself, which has more employees than at any other time in history. Congress has demonstrated no serious concern for reform. Presently, the voice of criticism is Congress criticizing the Administration or vice versa, but there is no evidence that either has any earnest intention of putting its house in order.

In my judgment, only aroused public opinion will force the political leaders of both parties to be more responsive to a desire for more effective government. While I think the report reads well, the political environment of Washington will limit its effectiveness. It may even be an expensive waste of time, if we really expect any changes as a result of the report.

Page 9—By FRANKLIN A. LINDSAY:

I support the recommendations of the report but believe that it gives inadequate recognition to the essentially political process by which a democracy selects among competing programs. Such decisions necessarily involve the resolution, through elected representatives, of the conflicts and inconsistencies inherent in the process of choosing goals and setting priorities. The administrative process, to which this report is largely directed, plays an important but secondary role.

Page 37—By RICHARD C. GERSTENBERG:

In general, I would question the imposition of special taxes or use charges as desirable social policy. With respect to items that pollute, our main effort should not be to limit consumption but rather to take positive steps to improve the environment. Past history shows us that *ad hoc* taxation tends to be ill-applied. Moreover, such taxation is likely to continue in effect even though its original purpose no longer exists.

Page 39—By RICHARD C. GERSTENBERG:

I would only add that when the private sector is asked to operate projects for the social good, that it is done with due consideration of all the costs involved—direct and indirect. Moreover, it is important to stress that the measurements of cost present very difficult methodological and conceptual problems. It is important that costs be accurately measured in relation to benefits. Without this, there is the risk that the public will expect more of both government and private business than either can deliver on an economically feasible basis.

64.

Appendix A

"Bandaging
the Bureaucracy
in Plenty of Red Tape"

By Art Buchwald
From *The Washington Post,*
July 1, 1971

WASHINGTON.

Congressman Jim Wright of Texas has held hearings on red tape in the federal government.

The hearings were inspired by some statistics his staff dug up including the fact that whereas in 1966 it took 79 days to process a public works grant for hard hit unemployment areas, it now takes 348 days.

A small business loan that once took 125 days to process now takes 309.

A federal highway program which once took six months to start after the plans were formulated now takes six years.

The big question that Congressman Wright has been trying to answer is: "How does the government manage to do it?"

*   *   *

What Congressman Wright doesn't know is that there is an entire government department devoted to finding new and more efficient ways of delaying federal programs.

One of its major trouble shooters is Archie Falstaff, who has the title of Inspector General, Red Tape and Paper Shuffling Division GS 4.

Archie told me that thanks to modern technology and communications, he has been able to triple the amount of paperwork in almost every branch of the government.

"Our secret," he said, "is having the wrong people in the right place at the wrong time. The more people you have involved in a federal project the more chance you have of making it ineffectual. But it's not a question of bodies. You have to watch and make sure that no one in the organization has the authority to make a decision.

"For example, I had a case a few months ago concerning air pollution. We noticed that universities and colleges were being given grants for research in air pollution without any difficulty, and we smelled a rat. So we infiltrated the department and discovered an ecological nut who was okaying the grants without sending them upstairs for future study, which usually takes a couple of years.

"We closed the loophole by making a regulation that 40 people, none of them involved in air pollution, had to unanimously approve any federal money spent for research. Since then not one school has qualified for a grant."

"I hope you took care of the troublemaker," I said.

"He's now working in the mailroom. Sometimes, though, we run into a situation where no one is at fault.

"Several months ago, a man whose laundry burned down came to the Small Business Administration for a loan. He presented references from his bank and filled out all the forms. Because everything seemed in order the bureaucrat in charge gave him the loan in less than six months.

"This was unheard of, and we decided to have a full investigation. We discovered the fault was not with the bureaucrat but with the forms, which were much too short and easy to understand.

"So we put our people on it and developed a new form, which was three times as long and so complicated no small businessman could fill it out without making 20 mistakes. Now that they're using the new forms we've quadrupled the time it takes to process an SBA loan."

*   *   *

"That was good planning," I said.

"I believe our greatest contribution to government red tape in the last few years is that we've seen to it that no single department has the final decision on any program.

"Suppose a mayor of a city comes to Washington to get federal money for a summer program. Our rules are that he can't get the money until winter.

"We'll send him to one department, where he'll be shunted off to another, who after making recommendations will pass it on to a third department, who will throw it back to the first. If the mayor keeps bugging us and insisting on the money, we'll take him to court."

65.

Appendix B

1969 GOVERNMENT PURCHASES
of GOODS AND SERVICES *(in billions of dollars)[a]*

	Federal		State and Local
	National Defense	*Non-Defense*	
TOTAL	**78.8**	**22.6**	**110.8**
Compensation of employees	32.1	10.0	61.5
Purchases from business	46.7	12.6	49.3
SELECTED NON-DEFENSE FUNCTIONS			
Education:	**0.9**		**47.4**
Compensation of employees	b		33.6
Purchases from business	b		13.8
Health, labor and welfare	**3.9**		**26.5**
Transportation	**1.8** [c]		**16.3**[c]
Housing and community development	**1.0**		**1.2**
Agriculture and agricultural resources	**2.4**		**1.2**
Natural resources	**2.5**		**3.0**

a. These amounts have been rounded.

b. Not available.

c. Government enterprise operated at deficit of $.2 billion at federal level and $.9 billion at state and local level, financed by public subsidy.

Source: Data from Survey of Current Business, *Vol. 50, No. 7 (July 1970), p. 34, Table 3.10; p. 35, Table 3.11.*

Appendix C

Program overview summaries have been under development within the Office of Management and Budget for several years. This appendix contains examples of such summaries presented before the Joint Economic Committee.[1]

Table C-1 covers a wide range of existing health programs; Table C-2 focuses on several alternative ways of improving the delivery of health services. Such summaries are neither intended nor appropriate for supporting conclusions about the merits of programs. Their purpose is to raise questions as a basis for choosing areas for intensive program analysis. This is especially true of the benefit/cost ratios.

The last two columns of Appendix Table C-1 should be interpreted as a tentative and gross approximation of program benefits. The "subsidy value" reflects, generally, the difference between the cost to the recipient of the service provided through, or with the assistance of the government program, and the cost to him without it. The benefit that enters the benefit/cost ratio is intended to reflect the value of the services provided by the program, regardless of whether those services are provided at less than cost. Both require the assumption that it is possible to estimate the market value of the services either by analysis or by comparison with a substitute actually available through the market.

Appendix C-3 provides a geographic summary of expenditure patterns of government programs, together with a summary of the distribution of population. It makes possible a rough appreciation of variations in per capital expenditures over geographic subdivisions.

Attempts have been made in the Office of Management and Budget to develop such summaries in each of the functional areas of federal activities (see Appendix E for a definition of functional areas). Data deficiencies have been severe in many of the areas, particularly for estimating program benefits.

---

[1]/U.S. Congress. Joint Economic Committee. Subcommittee on Economy in Government, *Economic Analysis and the Efficiency of Government.* Hearings, Ninety-first Congress, First Session (Washington, D.C.: U.S. Government Printing Office, 1970), Part 3, pp. 736-738, 703, 749. The tables were presented by Jack W. Carlson, Assistant Director for Program Evaluation, U.S. Office of Management and Budget.

PRELIMINARY HEALTH OVERVIEW – Disease Prevention and Control

Agency and expenditure purpose	Estimated expenses, 1970 (millions)	Number of units fiscal year 1970	Age −21	Age 21 to 55	Age 55+	Negro	White	Other	Income −$4,000	Income $4,000 to $9,999	Income $10,000+	Location cc ≥ 250,000	cc ≤ 250,000	Other urban	Rural	Subsidy Value	B/Ce
BIOMEDICAL RESEARCH																	
HEW:																	
Basic	$479.6	(?)	41	41	18	11	88	1	30	49	21	22	21	27	30	0	
Targeted	629.2	(?)	14	25	61	14	85	1	29	44	27	19	21	26	33	0	
AEC:																	
Basic	83.9	(?)	41	41	18	11	88	1	30	49	21	22	21	27	30	0	
Targeted	16.4	(?)	6	17	78	11	88	1	17	43	39	18	0	0	0	0	
NASA:																	
Basic	45.6	(?)	0	0	0	0	0	0	0	0	0	0	0	0	0	0	
Targeted	65.0	(?)	0	0	0	0	0	0	0	0	0	0	0	0	0	0	
VA:																	
Basic	4.9	(?)	41	41	18	11	88	1	30	49	21	22	21	27	30	0	
Targeted	54.8	(?)	0	0	100	15	83	2	18	39	43	15	21	27	37	0	
DOD:																	
Basic	48.9	(?)	41	41	18	11	88	1	30	49	21	22	21	27	30	0	
Targeted	55.4	(?)	18	34	48	15	83	2	29	46	25	21	21	26	32	0	
Agriculture:																	
Basic	24.2	(?)	41	41	18	11	88	1	18	58	21	22	21	27	30	0	
Targeted	14.6	(?)	38	43	19	11	88	1	28	42	30	17	21	26	35	0	
NSF: Basic	24.4	(?)	41	41	18	11	88	1	18	58	21	22	21	27	30	0	
BIOMEDICAL RESEARCH FACILITIES																	
HEW:																	
Direct	15.1	(?)	41	41	18	11	88	1	30	49	21	22	21	27	30	0	
Federal share	96.3	(?)	41	41	18	11	88	1	30	49	21	22	21	27	30	0	
Agriculture: Direct	4.0	(?)	38	43	19	11	88	1	28	42	30	17	21	26	35	0	
VA: Direct	5.8	(?)	0	0	100	15	83	2	18	39	43	15	15	27	37	0	
AEC: Direct	3.6	(?)	41	41	18	11	88	1	30	49	21	22	21	27	30	0	
BIOMEDICAL MANPOWER																	
HEW:																	
Student support	118.4	15,000 studs	11	25	64	16	83	1	29	44	28	19	21	26	34	$4,813	
Institutional support		422 ed. inst															
National distribution			41	41	18	11	88	1	30	49	21	22	21	27	³ 30		1.00

[1] Benefit recipient characteristics

		Beds Added or modernized:															
HOSPITAL CONSTRUCTION																	
HEW: Direct	5.2	0	39	44	17	6	34	57	48	43	9	40	0	9	51	$14.50/pd	.50
Federal share	145.3	16,413	20	46	34	12	87	1	38	48	14	19	7	68	6	$5.75/pd	.50
VA: Direct	77.7	476	0	29	71	14	84	2	35	60	5	15	17	22	46	$14.50/pd	.50
DOD: Direct	58.1	600	38	47	15	17	82	1	37	44	19	(¹)	(³)	(³)	(²)		
NURSING HOMES CONSTRUCTION																	
HEW: Federal share	.9	300	0	7	93	4	96	0	60	35	5	15	4	64	17	$3.00/pd	1.00
VA: Direct		0	0	7	93	4	94	2	60	35	5	15	17	22	46	$7.00/pd	1.00
Federal share	3.2	795	0	7	93	4	94	2	60	35	5	15	17	22	46	$3.00/pd	1.00
CLINICS		Fac. added:															
HEW: Direct	2.7		39	44	17	6	37	57	48	43	9	40	0	9	51	$3.75/visit	1.00
Federal share		9,390	41	41	18	12	87	1	34	49	17	22	5	57	16	$1.25/visit	1.00
DOD: Direct	.1		38	47	15	17	82	1	37	44	19	(²)	(²)	(²)	(²)	$3.75/visit	1.00
PHYSICIAN MANPOWER																	
HEW: Student support	116.9	1,586 grad	35	42	23	8	91	1	23	50	27	24	23	27	26	$265/stud	1.9
Construction	80.7	439 spaces	35	42	23	8	91	1	23	50	27	24	23	27	26	$82/stud	1.9
DOD: Student support	14.6	1,590 grad	35	42	23	8	91	1	23	50	27	24	23	27	26	$8,000	1.9
DENTAL MANPOWER																	
HEW: Student support	30.8	1,743 grad	37	48	15	6	93	1	15	56	29	25	24	29	22	$265/stud	1.1
Construction	18.6	180 spaces	37	48	15	6	93	1	15	56	29	25	24	29	22	$60/stud	
NURSE MANPOWER																	
HEW: Student support	52.6	14,369 grad	40	42	18	11	88	1	21	49	30	26	26	26	22	$100/stud	1.6
Construction	16.8	570 spaces	40	42	18	11	88	1	21	49	30	26	26	26	22	00/stud	00
DOD: Student support	2.4	1,505 grad	38	47	15	17	82	1	37	44	19	(³)	(³)	(³)	(³)	$3,000/stud	1.6
OTHER HEALTH PROF.																	
HEW: Student support	74.3	5,862 grad	41	41	18	11	88	1	21	49	30	22	21	27	30		
Construction	3.7	149 spaces															
DOD: Student support	3.6	903 grad															
AEC: Student support	.6	28 grad															

1. Percent distributions are approximate, not official agency estimates.   2. Not applicable.   3. Based on 1960 census data.

continued on next page

Agency and expenditure purpose	Estimated expenses, 1970 (millions)	Number of units fiscal year 1970	Age			Race			Income			Location				Benefits	
			−21	21 to 55	55+	Negro	White	Other	−$4,000	$4,000 to $9,999	$10,000+	cc ≥ 250,000	cc ≤ 250,000	Other urban	Rural	Subsidy Value	B/Ce
OTHER HEALTH TRAINING																	
HEW: Student support	$130.8	31,020 train															
DOD: Student support	103.4	2,444 train															
VA: Student support	95.4	train															
Labor: Student support	35.4	19,730 train															
PROVISION OF HOSPITAL SERVICES		Patients:															
HEW:																	
Direct	93.4	130,604	39	44	17	6	37	57	48	43	9	40	0	9	51	$335/pat	1.80
Finance	6,352.5	6,593,840	10	7	83	11	88	1	60	29	11	16	21	27	36	$181/pat	.66
DOD:																	
Direct	791.9	1,354,105	31	69	.4	17	82	1	74	22	4	(?)	(?)	(?)	(?)	$442/pat	2.60
Finance	183.4	270,829	38	47	15	17	82	1	74	22	4	(?)	(?)	(?)	(?)	$348/pat	1.90
VA:																	
Direct	1,100.9	775,000	0	29	71	14	84	2	35	60	5	10	10	34	46	$313/pat	.98
Finance	15.7	24,916	0	57	43	14	84	2	37	44	19	10	10	35	45	$423/pat	1.50
OTHER INPATIENT SERVICES																	
HEW: Finance	936.4	20,107,584	10	7	83	11	88	1	60	29	11	16	21	27	36	$181/pat	.66
DOD: Finance	.02	806,429	38	47	15	17	82	1	74	22	4	(?)	(?)	(?)	(?)	$348/pat	1.90
VA:																	
Direct	62.3	1,382,518	0	29	71	14	84	2	35	60	5	10	10	34	46	$313/pat	.98
Finance	33.1		0	57	43	14	84	2	37	44	19	10	10	35	45	$423/pat	1.50
OUTPATIENT SERVICES		Visits:															
HEW:																	
Direct	38.2	1,919,091	39	44	17	6	37	57	48	43	9	40	0	9	51	$20/visit	1.80
Finance	2,936.8	1,415,920	10	7	83	11	88	1	46	41	13	17	23	27	33	do	.66
DOD:																	
Direct	670.6	49,382,747	31	69	.4	17	82	1	74	22	4	(?)	(?)	(?)	(?)	do	2.60
Finance	26.3	67,634	38	47	15	17	82	1	74	22	4	(?)	(?)	(?)	(?)	do	1.90
VA: Direct	177.4	6,277,328	2	70	28	14	84	2	24	58	18	10	10	35	45	$25/visit	1.90
OEO: Direct			60	23	17	65	20	15	95	5	0	45	15	20	20	$20/visit	1.90
National distribution			41	41	18	11	88	1	21	49	30	22	21	27	30		1.43

Benefit recipient characteristics[1]

1. Percent distributions are approximate, not official agency estimates.　2. Not applicable.　3. Based on 1960 census data.

Appendix C-2

COMPARISON OF ALTERNATIVES to the Hill-Burton Program

Hill-Burton program and alternatives	Estimated expenditures fiscal year 1970 (millions)	Benefit cost ratio[1]	Age			Income			Race		Location cc 250,000+	Suburbs of cc 250,000+	Other Urban	Rural
			−21	21-55	55+	−$4,000	$4,000 to $9,999	$10,000 +	Negro	White				
1. Hill-Burton hospitals	$145.3	0.6	20	46	34	38	48	14	12	87	19	7	68	6
2. Neighborhood health facilities	84.8	(1.4)	60	23	17	95	5	0	65	20	45	15	20	20
3. Increase in physicians	133.0	1.9	35	42	23	24	50	27	8	91	24	23	27	26
4. Family planning	143.0	10.0	59	41	0	90	10	0	35	60	29	15	28	28
5. Maternal and Infant care centers (Children's Bureau)	62.8	(.8)	43	57	0	100	0	0	60	35	29	15	28	28
6. Enrichment of foods commonly eaten by low-income groups		(8.0)	44	30	26	90	10	0	32	68	17	9	36	38
National Distribution			41	41	18	21	49	30	11	88	22	21	27	30

Characteristics of beneficiaries

1. Parentheses indicate preliminary nature of estimates.
Note: Some data had explanatory information in the original table.

Appendix C-3

GEOGRAPHIC SUMMARY of
Expenditure Patterns of Government Programs

	Percent of population	Percent of Federal expenditures
Poorest counties	10	6
Richest counties	10	14
Slowest growing counties	10	11
Fastest growing counties	10	12
SMSA's more than 1,000,000 (1966)	37	44
SMSA's less than 1,000,000 (1966)	30	31
Non-SMSA urban counties	11	10
Rural counties	22	16
Central cities	13	19
Suburbs	8	9

Appendix D

AN EXAMPLE OF
COST-EFFECTIVENESS ANALYSIS

This appendix presents an example of cost-effectiveness analysis performed in the Department of Health, Education, and Welfare. The discussion is reproduced from a paper by Robert N. Grosse, "Problems of Resource Allocation in Health," published as part of a compendium prepared by the Joint Economic Committee.[1] It was selected for its clear summarization of the conclusions and some of the consequences of two sets of analyses of alternative resource allocations for health programs. Both are in the form of cost-effectiveness analyses, approximating benefits in terms such as "deaths averted" and "handicaps prevented," as well as in dollar terms. Excerpts from Mr. Grosse's paper follow:

Disease Control Programs

One of the first analytical studies of the PPB era at DHEW was a study of disease control programs. Considerable work had been done during the last ten years in estimating the economic costs of particular diseases. Among the best known of these are Rashi Fein's *Economics of Mental Illness,* Burton Weisbrod's *Economics of Public Health* in which he estimated the costs of cancer, tuberculosis, and poliomyelitis, Herbert Klarman's paper on syphilis control programs, and Dorothy Rice's studies covering the international classification of diseases. A generation earlier Dublin and Lotka's classic explored the impact of disease and disability and their relation to changes in earning power. The economic implications of disability were, of course, a matter of central interest in the area of workmen's compensation insurance. It was not surprising, then, that when systematic quantitative analysis of government programs and policies began to spread from defense to civilian applications, one of the first analytical studies was a study of disease control programs.

The basic concept of the study was a simple one. HEW supports (or could support) a number of categorical disease control programs, whose objectives are to save lives or to prevent disability by controlling specific diseases. The study was an attempt to answer the question: If additional money were to be allocated to disease control programs, which programs would show the highest payoff in terms of lives saved and disability prevented per dollar spent? The study defines "disease" liberally. Motor vehicle accidents were included along with tuberculosis, syphilis, cancer, and arthritis.

---

[1]/Robert N. Grosse, "Problems of Resource Allocation in Health," in U.S. Congress. Joint Economic Committee, Subcommittee on Economy in Government, *The Analysis and Evaluation of Public Expenditures: The PPB System; A Compendium of Papers* (Washington, D.C.: U.S. Government Printing Office, 1969), pp. 1209-1215, 1219-1220.

Figure D-1: CANCER CONTROL PROGRAM: 1968-1972

	Uterine-cervix	Breast	Head and neck	Colon-rectum
Grant costs (in thousands)	$97,750	$17,750	$13,250	$13,300
Number of examinations (in thousands)	9,363	2,280	609	662
Cost per examination	$10.44	$7.79	$21.76	$20.10
Examinations per case found	87.5	167.3	620.2	496.0
Cancer cases found	107,045	13,628	982	1,334
Cost per case found	$913	$1,302	$13,493	$9,970
Cancer deaths averted	44,084	2,936	303	288
Cost per death averted	$2,217	$6,046	$43,729	$46,181

I'm talking here not about research, but where a technology exists and the problem is whether to put the same, more, or less federal funds behind these control programs to support activities in hospitals, states, and communities. The question we address is where should we allocate the resources available for this purpose.

Figure D-1 illustrates the approach to one set of diseases, cancer. We looked at cancer of the uterine cervix, breast, head and neck and colon-rectum. We estimated cost per examination, and the probable number of examinations that would be required for each case found. From this was derived the number of cases that would be found for an expenditure level, and estimates of the cost per case found. An estimate was made of the number of deaths that could be averted by the treatment following the detection of the cancers and then we calculated the cost per death averted which ranged from about $2,200 in the case of cervical cancer up to $40,000 to $45,000 in the case of head and neck and colon-rectum cancer.

On the vertical axis of Figure D-2 we have plotted the program costs; this includes the cost of the treatment in addition to the federal detection program. On the horizontal axis estimates of deaths averted are ordered by increase in cost per death averted in each program. Segments of the curve identified to each disease cover the extent of the program which it was estimated could be mounted in the years 1968-72 before running into sharply increasing costs. In concept, the cervical cancer curve is cut off where costs become higher than the breast cancer program, etc. From this analysis one might say that if there is only available $50 million, cervical cancer should get all the funds. If we have $115 million, then breast cancer control programs look quite competitive. Head and neck and colon-rectum cancer detection program as major control programs did not look attractive when viewed in this context. The analysts recommended that they concentrate on research and development.

74.

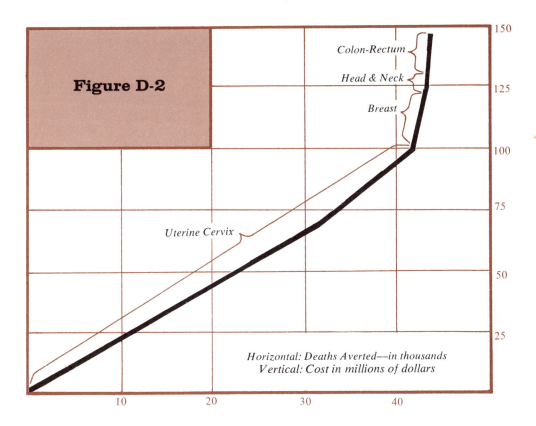

Figure D-2

Colon-Rectum

Head & Neck

Breast

Uterine Cervix

Horizontal: Deaths Averted—in thousands
Vertical: Cost in millions of dollars

The same kind of analysis was performed for each of the five programs studied (Figure D-3). There seemed to be a very high potential payoff for certain educational programs in motor vehicle injury prevention trying to persuade people to use seatbelts, not to walk in front of a car, and so on. And then as we move up this curve, again ordered by cost of averting death we begin adding the others. This particular criterion, deaths averted, was not completely satisfactory. The number of fatalities attributed to arthritis were negligible. Secondly, there is the question, did it matter who died? Did it matter whether it was a 30-year-old mother or a 40-year-old father of a family or a 75-year-old grandfather? On Figure D-4, dollar savings summing avoided medical treatments and a crude estimate of the average (discounted) lifetime earnings saved are plotted as a variable in place of deaths averted. There are two changes in results: Cervical cancer and syphilis control programs change places in priority order, and we are able to introduce the arthritis program.

Allocations of resources to programs are developed from such analyses by using information such as this and the preceding charts as an additional insight to give an additional feel for what were relatively high-priority and what were relatively low-priority programs, and then to feed these insights into the decision-making process which also considers existing commitments, the political situation, feasible changes in the rates of spending, the ability to get people moving on programs, and so on.

These studies were not greeted with universal acclaim. Criticisms focused on a number of problems. First, with almost no exception the conclusions were based on average relationships. That is, the total benefits were divided by the total costs.

75.

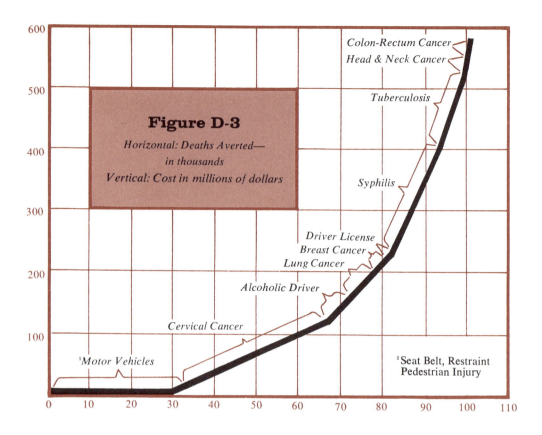

Figure D-3

Horizontal: Deaths Averted—
in thousands
Vertical: Cost in millions of dollars

Colon-Rectum Cancer
Head & Neck Cancer

Tuberculosis

Syphilis

Driver License
Breast Cancer
Lung Cancer

Alcoholic Driver

Cervical Cancer

[1]Motor Vehicles

[1]Seat Belt, Restraint
Pedestrian Injury

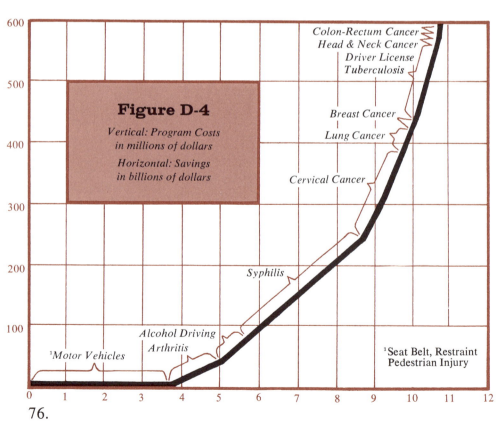

Figure D-4

Vertical: Program Costs
in millions of dollars

Horizontal: Savings
in billions of dollars

Colon-Rectum Cancer
Head & Neck Cancer
Driver License
Tuberculosis

Breast Cancer
Lung Cancer

Cervical Cancer

Syphilis

Alcohol Driving
Arthritis

[1]Motor Vehicles

[1]Seat Belt, Restraint
Pedestrian Injury

76.

There was little evidence of what the actual impact of increasing or decreasing programs by small amounts might be. If we actually believed the average ratios to be valid at the margin, ought we not to put all our funds into the program with the highest benefit-cost or deaths averted per dollar ratios?

Let me illustrate with a hypothetical example how such marginal information might be used to determine the preferred mix of disease control programs. Assume that we can determine as in the following tables the number of lives saved by different expenditures on disease A and disease B:

Disease A

Expenditures	Lives Saved
$ 500,000	360
$1,000,000	465

Disease B

$ 500,000	200
$1,000,000	270

If we only knew the effect of spending $1 million, we might opt for a program where all our money was spent on controlling disease A, as we could save 465 lives instead of 270 if we spent it all on disease B. Similarly, if we only knew the effects of programs of a half million dollars, we would probably prefer A, as we'd save 360 rather than only 200 lives.

But if we knew the results for expenditures of both half a million and 1 million dollars in each program, we would quickly see that spending half our money in each program was better than putting it all in one assuming we have $1 million available:

Our calculations would be:

Expenditures			Lives saved
$1,000,000 on A			465
$1,000,000 on B			270
$1,000,000	{ $500,000 on A 360		
	{ $500,000 on B .... 200 }		560

But suppose we had still more discrete data, as in the following tables which give us the effect of each hundred thousand dollars spent on each control program:

Disease A

Expenditures	Lives Saved
$ 100,000	100
$ 200,000	180
$ 300,000	250
$ 400,000	310
$ 500,000	360
$ 600,000	400
$ 700,000	430
$ 800,000	450
$ 900,000	460
$1,000,000	465

77.

Disease B

$ 100,000	50
$ 200,000	95
$ 300,000	135
$ 400,000	170
$ 500,000	200
$ 600,000	225
$ 700,000	240
$ 800,000	255
$ 900,000	265
$1,000,000	270

We could then spend the million dollars even more effectively:

Lives saved

$1,000,000 $\begin{cases} \$600,000 \text{ on A} \dots\dots 400 \\ \$400,000 \text{ on B} \dots\dots 170 \end{cases}$ 570

The lack of marginal data resulted from both a lack of such data for most programs, together with a lack of economic sophistication on the part of the Public Health Service analysts who performed the studies. Despite the theoretical shortcomings, the results were useful when applied with some common sense.

Practical obstacles of existing commitments made it almost impossible to recommend *reductions* in any program. So the decisions dealt with the allocation of modest increments.

In the case of oral and colon-rectum cancers, the average cost per death averted seemed so high that the Department recommended emphasis on research and development, rather than a control program to demonstrate and extend current technology.

In cervical cancer, investigation indicated a sizable number of hospitals in low socioeconomic areas without detection programs which would be willing to establish these if supported by federal funds. The unit costs of increasing the number of hospitals seemed to be the same as that of those already in the program. Shifting the approach to reach out for additional women in the community would increase costs per examination, but not so high as to change the relative position of this program. At most, it raised costs to about those of the breast cancer control program.

Despite the seeming high potential payoff of some of the motor vehicle programs, there was considerable uncertainty about the success. As a consequence recommendations were for small programs with a large emphasis on evaluation for use in future decisions. The same philosophy was applied to the arthritis program.

What resulted then, was a setting of priorities for additional funding, based on the analytical results, judgment about their reliability, and practical considerations.

A second type of criticism of the analysis described above was concerned with the criteria, especially the calculation of benefits. They were considered inadequate in that they paid attention to economic productivity alone, and omitted other considerations. In particular, they were thought to discriminate against the old who might be past employment years, and women whose earnings were relatively low. It was also feared that the logic, if vigorously pursued, would penalize not only health programs for the aged such as the newly launched medicare, but also programs aimed at assisting the poor whose relative earning power is low by definition.

78.

In actual practice in the programs studied, these concerns were only hypothetical. The programs for cervical and breast cancer looked to be good despite their being for women. As for the poor, most of the programs considered, especially cervical cancer, syphilis, and tuberculosis were aimed primarily at them, and projects were usually located to serve low-income residents.

Another type of objection was raised not against the technique of analysis, but against its being done at all. Choices among diseases to be controlled and concern with costs of saving lives can be viewed as contrary to physicians' attitudes in the care of an individual patient. Yet, such decisions are made, analysis or no. Prior decisions on allocations to various health problems rested upon a combination of perception of the magnitude of the problem and the political strength organized to secure funding, e.g., the National Tuberculosis Association.

The disease control cost-benefit analyses suggest that additional considerations are very relevant. Given scarce resources (and if they are not, there is no allocation problem), one ought to estimate the costs of achieving improvements in health. If we can save more lives by applying resources to a small (in numbers affected) problem than a large one, we ought to consider doing so.

Maternal and Child Health Programs

In regard to maternal and child care programs the stated goal was to make needed maternal and child health services available and accessible to all, in particular to all expectant mothers and children in health depressed areas. Health depressed areas could be characterized as areas with excessive infant mortality rates. There is no universal index of good or bad health among children. Two measurable areas were selected—mortality and the prevalence of chronic handicapping conditions. Over a dozen possible programs aimed at reducing these were examined. On Figure D-5, three selected programs addressed to the problem of coverage of maternal and child health are illustrated, two of them comprehensive programs of care to expectant

Figure D-5: YEARLY EFFECTS per $10,000,000 EXPENDED in HEALTH-DEPRESSED AREAS

	Comprehensive programs		Case finding of treatment 0, 1, 3, 5, 7, 9
	to age 18	to age 5	
Maternal deaths prevented	1.6	3	
Premature births prevented	100-250	200-485	
Infant deaths prevented	40-60	85-120	
Mental retardation prevented	5-7	7-14	
Handicaps prevented or corrected by age 18:			
Vision problems: All	350	195	3,470
Amblyopia	60	119	1,140
Hearing loss: All	90	70	7,290
Binaural	6	5	60
Other physical handicaps	200	63	1,470

mothers and children. This table shows the annual effects of spending the same amount of money, $10 million a year, in different ways. The analysts examined comprehensive care programs covering up to age 18 and up to age 5 with estimates based on the best assumptions derived from the literature and advisers on the probabilities of prevention of maternal deaths, premature deaths, infant deaths, and mental retardation, and handicapping conditions prevented or corrected by age 18. They also looked at a program of early case finding and assured treatment which focused on children at ages 4 days and again every other year until they were 9. Expending the same amounts, where you put the money yields different results. With respect to reduction of infant mortality, several other programs had higher payoffs than these. For example, a program of intensive care units for high-risk newborns was estimated to reduce annually 367 deaths if we put all our money in that basket—it would cost about $27 thousand per infant death prevented. The programs shown cost about four times that, but they do other good things too.

The HEW analysts also looked at programs with a given amount of money aimed at reducing the number of children who will have decayed and unfilled teeth by age 18. Fluoridation programs in communities which do not possess this, will, for the same amount of money, give us close to 300,000 fewer children in this condition, compared to 18,000 or 44,000 fewer in other programs noted. Fluoridation looks like a very attractive program. It was so attractive that it could be inferred that a program as cheap as this is not being inhibited by lack of financial support by the federal government; there are other factors at work.

Reduction in Number of 18-Year-Olds with Decayed and Unfilled Teeth
per $10,000,000 Expended in Health-Depressed Areas

Fluoridation	294,000
Comprehensive dental care without fluoridation	18,000
Comprehensive dental care with fluoridation	44,000

One other program, additional funds on family planning, looked like a very good way not only to reduce the number of infant deaths, but also the rate of infant mortality in high-risk communities.

Despite the information difficulties, several conclusions emerged clearly from the study. *Two of these conclusions resulted in new legislation being requested from Congress.** First, it seemed clear that a program of early casefindings and treatment of handicapping conditions would have considerable payoff. It was also clear that if the large number of children who do not now have access to good medical care were to be provided with pediatric services, an acute shortage of doctors would be precipitated. Ways have to be found to use medical manpower more efficiently. The Social Security Amendments of 1967 include provision for programs of early casefinding and treatment of defects and chronic conditions in children, and for research and demonstration programs in the training and use of physician assistants.

These condensed discussions of some of HEW's applications of cost-benefit analysis to disease-control programs illustrate both the usefulness and limitations of such analyses for decisionmaking. Issues are sharpened, and quantitative estimates are developed to reduce the decisionmakers' uncertainty about costs and effects. Nevertheless, the multiplicity of dimensions of output, and their basic incommensurabilities both with costs and the outputs of other claimants for public expenditure still requires the use of value judgments and political consensus.

*Italics added.

80.

Appendix E

Alternative Budget Classification Systems

   This appendix illustrates the three basic budget classification systems used by the federal government in the presentation of the fiscal year 1972 Budget. All the tables in this appendix have been reproduced from or summarized from the Budget document.[1] Figure E-1 shows federal outlays and obligational authority by functional category. Figure E-2 shows, in greater functional detail, the breakdown among federal departments and agencies of obligational authority for the functional category, "health." Figure E-3 summarizes the Department of Health, Education, and Welfare budget by the major organizational units receiving appropriations, and delegated financial responsibility. Figure E-4 shows selected appropriations to the Health Services and Mental Health Administration. Figure E-5 shows the program structure for the Department of Health, Education, and Welfare.

Figure E-1: SUMMARY OF BUDGET OUTLAYS BY FUNCTION *(in millions of dollars)*

Function	Outlays			Recommended budget authority for 1972
	1970 actual	1971 estimate	1972 estimate	
National defense	80,295	76,443	77,512	80,211
International affairs and finance	3,570	3,586	4,032	5,108
Space research and technology	3,749	3,368	3,151	3,270
Agriculture and rural development	6,201	5,262	5,804	6,363
Natural resources	2,480	2,636	4,243	4,907
Commerce and transportation	9,310	11,442	10,937	12,320
Community development and housing	2,965	3,858	4,495	4,470
Education and manpower	7,289	8,300	8,808	10,391
Health	12,995	14,928	16,010	20,384
Income security	43,790	55,546	60,739	66,892
Veterans benefits and services	8,677	9,969	10,644	10,991
Interest	18,312	19,433	19,687	19,687
General government	3,336	4,381	4,970	5,335
Allowances:				
Added amount for revenue sharing			4,019	4,106
Pay increase (excluding Department of Defense)		500	1,000	1,050
Contingencies		300	950	1,250
Undistributed intragovernmental transactions:				
Employer share, employee retirement	—2,444	—2,486	—2,461	—2,461
Interest received by trust funds	—3,936	—4,711	—5,310	—5,310
Total	196,588	212,755	229,232	248,965
Expenditure account	194,456	211,143	228,286	246,927
Loan account	2,131	1,611	946	2,038

[1]/Data from U.S. Office of Management and Budget, *The Budget of the United States Government, Fiscal Year 1972*, pp. 81, 548, 300-327, 301-305; and U.S. Office of Management and Budget, *Special Analyses, Budget of the United States Government, Fiscal Year 1972*, pp. 294-295.

Figure E-2: BUDGET AUTHORITY
BY FUNCTION AND AGENCY *(in millions of dollars)*

Function and department or other unit	New Obligational Authority			Loan Authority		
	1970 actual	1971 estimate	1972 estimate	1970 actual	1971 estimate	1972 estimate
650 HEALTH 651 Development of health resources:						
Department of Health, Education, and Welfare	2,014	2,337	2,418	5	10	—*
652 Providing or financing medical services:						
Department of Health, Education, and Welfare	10,587	13,937	17,147			
653 Prevention and control of health problems:						
Department of Health, Education, and Welfare	495	582	621			
Environmental Protection Agency	117	147	216			
Other independent agencies: Temporary study commissions		1				
Total 653	611	730	837			
Deductions for offsetting receipts:						
Proprietary receipts from the public	—6	—2	—18			
Total HEALTH	**13,207**	**17,003**	**20,384**	**5**	**10**	**—***

Less than $500 thousand.

82.

Figure E-3: DEPARTMENT OF HEALTH, EDUCATION, AND WELFARE BUDGET

(by major organizational units)

Organizational Unit	Fiscal Year 1972 Budget Authority (in millions of dollars) [a]
Food and Drug Administration	95.2
Environmental Health Service	[b]
Health Services and Mental Health Administration	1,632.6
National Institutes of Health	1,889.5
Office of Education	6,126.4
Social and Rehabilitation Service	12,089.4
Social Security Administration:	
Federal Funds	2,850.2
Trust Funds	56,127.5
Special Institutions	80.0
Office of Child Development	392.7
Departmental Management	56.0
Welfare Reform and Community Services	742.8
Total Federal Funds	**25,954.8**
Total Trust Funds	**56,127.7**
Adjustments (Deduct)	−3,292.8
Total Department of Health, Education, and Welfare	**78,789.7**

a. *These amounts have been rounded.*
b. *Transferred to Environmental Protection Agency and other appropriations within the Department of Health, Education, and Welfare.*

Figure E-4: SELECTED APPROPRIATIONS to the HEALTH SERVICES and MENTAL HEALTH ADMINISTRATION

Appropriation	Fiscal Year 1972 Budget Authority (in millions of dollars)[a]
Mental health:	
Development of health resources	238.4
Prevention and control of health problems	183.7
Saint Elizabeth's Hospital	21.3
Health services research and development	61.5
Comprehensive health planning and services:	
Development of health resources	28.7
Prevention and control of health problems	223.1
Maternal and child health	326.4
Regional medical programs:	
Development of health resources	46.2
Prevention and control of health problems	6.2
Disease control	78.0
Medical facilities construction	138.7
National health statistics	15.3
Retirement pay and medical benefits for commissioned officers (of the Public Health Service)	23.2
Buildings and facilities	5.1
Office of the Administrator	11.8
Indian health services	137.6
Indian health facilities	18.8
Other appropriations	68.7
Total Health Services and Mental Health Administration	**1,632.7**

a. These amounts have been rounded.

84.

Department of Health, Education, and Welfare Program Structure

The broad objectives of the Department are reflected by four program categories—Education, Health, Social and rehabilitation services, and Income security—and their associated subcategories.

Increases in budget authority requested for Education programs reflect two major areas of emphasis: emergency school assistance for desegregating local education agencies; and the revision of existing student aid programs to insure that no qualified student who wants to go to college will be barred by lack of funds.

Budget authority increases requested for programs which support Health objectives are essentially contained in two health financing programs: Medicare and Medicaid. While the increases reflect changes in the cost and use of health services, they also take into account counter-balancing legislative proposals to help solve the problems of rising medical cost and overutilization of hospital services.

The requested increases in total budget authority in support of Social and rehabilitation services fall equally into the social services grants to States (part of public assistance program) and the work incentive (WIN) program which includes child care.

Total budget authority requested for programs which support Income security objectives increases by $8 billion. This includes a request of $580 million for the welfare reform proposed legislation. The remainder is accounted for by maintenance payment grants and Social Security OASDI programs. Maintenance payment grants to States—a part of the public assistance program—rises by $1.8 billion. Budget authority for Social Security OASDI programs increases by $3.3 billion as a result of proposed legislation. It should be noted that for these programs budget authority is the "income to the trust fund"; tables specifying program outlays should be used to determine 1972 program costs for these programs.

Figure E-5: PROGRAM DISTRIBUTION of Budget Authority, Department of Health, Education, and Welfare *(in millions of dollars)*

Program category and subcategory	1972 estimate
Education:	
Development of basic skills	4,070.6
Development of vocational and occupational skills	433.6
Development of academic and professional skills	1,980.4
Library and community development	19.5
General research (nonallocable research)	34.6
General support	49.0
Category total	**6,587.7**

continued on next page

continued from preceding page

Program category and subcategory	1972 estimate
Health:	
Development of health resources	2,584.9
Prevention and control of health problems	367.6
Provision of health services	19,144.6
General support	64.7
Category total	**22,161.9**
Social and rehabilitation services:	
Improving individual capability for self-support	1,001.4
Improving the social functioning of individuals and families	1,013.4
General development of social and rehabilitation resources	108.8
General support	41.3
Category total	**2,164.9**
Income security:	
Aged assistance	29,551.7
Disability assistance	5,927.1
Other individual and family support	15,215.3
Increasing knowledge	11.0
General support	409.6
Category total	**51,114.6**
Executive direction and management (departmental management)	56.0
Total distributed to programs above	**82,085.0**
Net deductions for interfund transactions and receipts from the public not distributed above	−3,295.3
Total budget authority, Department of Health, Education, and Welfare	**78,789.7**

86.

PUBLICATION ORDER FORM

To order CED publications please indicate number in column entitled "# Copies Desired." Then mail this order form and check for total amount in envelope to Distribution Division, CED, 477 Madison Ave., New York 10022.

STATEMENTS ON NATIONAL POLICY *(paper bound)*

ORDER NUMBER   # COPIES DESIRED

43P .. IMPROVING FEDERAL PROGRAM PERFORMANCE $1.50 _____

Focuses attention on three major areas of concern about federal programs: (1) the choice of policy goals and program objectives, (2) the selection of programs that will achieve those objectives, and (3) the execution of the programs and the evaluation of their performance. Implicit in the changes recommended is the need for greater accountability by the federal government to the people.

42P .. SOCIAL RESPONSIBILITIES OF BUSINESS CORPORATIONS $1.50 _____

Develops a rationale for corporate involvement in solving such pressing social problems as urban blight, poverty, and pollution. Examines the need for the corporation to make its social responsibilities an integral part of its business objectives. Points out at the same time the proper limitations on such activities.

41P .. EDUCATION FOR THE URBAN DISADVANTAGED: From Preschool to Employment $1.50 _____

A comprehensive review of the current state of education for disadvantaged minorities; sets forth philosophical and operational principles which are imperative if the mission of the urban schools is to be accomplished successfully.

40P .. FURTHER WEAPONS AGAINST INFLATION $1.50 _____

Examines the problem of reconciling high employment and price stability. Maintains that measures to supplement general fiscal and monetary policies will be needed—including the use of voluntary wage-price (or "incomes") policies, as well as measures to change the structural and institutional environment in which demand policy operates.

39P .. MAKING CONGRESS MORE EFFECTIVE $1.00 _____

Points out the structural and procedural handicaps limiting the ability of Congress to respond to the nation's needs. Proposes a far-reaching Congressional reform program, including a sweeping realignment and democratization of the entire committee structure, fundamental changes in budgetary procedures, and broad measures to strengthen public confidence in the objectivity of Congress.

38P .. DEVELOPMENT ASSISTANCE TO SOUTHEAST ASIA $1.50 _____

Deals with the importance of external resources—financial, managerial, and technological, including public and private—to the development of Southeast Asia. The emphasis is on the special responsibility of the U.S., Japan, and Australia to contribute such resources to economic and social development of the region.

37P .. TRAINING AND JOBS FOR THE URBAN POOR $1.25 _____

Explores ways of abating poverty that arises from low wages and chronic unemployment or underemployment. Evaluates current manpower training and employment efforts by government and business. Recommends new government programs and the establishment of an experimental nonprofit Jobs Corporation to provide training and job opportunities for all those who want to work.

36P .. IMPROVING THE PUBLIC WELFARE SYSTEM $1.00 _____

Analyzes the national problem of poverty and the role played by the present welfare system. The statement recommends major changes in both the rationale and the administration of the public assistance program, with a view to establishing need as the sole criterion for coverage.

35P .. RESHAPING GOVERNMENT IN METROPOLITAN AREAS $1.00 _____

Recommends a two-level system of government for metropolitan areas: an area-wide level and a local level comprised of "community districts." Provides a brief description of problems in metropolitan areas which severely limit the quality of life and demonstrates the ways in which the existing governmental structure stands in the way of their solution.

34P .. ASSISTING DEVELOPMENT IN LOW-INCOME COUNTRIES $1.25 _____

Offers a sound rationale for public support of the U.S. economic assistance program and recommends a far-ranging set of priorities for U.S. Government policy.

33P .. NONTARIFF DISTORTIONS OF TRADE $1.00 _____

Examines the complex problem of dealing with nontariff distortions of trade arising from governmental measures that create special barriers to imports and incentives to exports.

32P .. FISCAL AND MONETARY POLICIES FOR STEADY ECONOMIC GROWTH $1.00 _____

Reexamines the role of fiscal and monetary policies in achieving the basic economic objectives of high employment, price stability, economic growth, and equilibrium in the nation's international payments.

31P .. FINANCING A BETTER ELECTION SYSTEM $1.00 _____

Urges comprehensive modernization of election and campaign procedures at national, state, and local levels. Proposes ways to reduce costs and spread them more widely through tax credits.

30P .. INNOVATION IN EDUCATION $1.00 _____

Examines the problems of the American schools, reviews educational goals and opportunities (including technological resources), and explores relative costs and benefits. Sets forth comprehensive recommendations for change.

SEE OTHER SIDE

ORDER NUMBER   # COPIES DESIRED

29P .. THE NATIONAL ECONOMY AND THE VIETNAM WAR $1.00   _____
      Shows how the nation has faltered in dealing with the economic impact of the rapid
      increase in government spending for Vietnam. Discusses the economic transition
      from war to peace.

28P .. MODERNIZING STATE GOVERNMENT $1.00   _____
      Recommends sweeping renovation of state governments and their constitutions. Pro-
      poses granting legislatures broad powers to deal with problems of a rapidly-changing
      era; strengthening executive capability through modern management methods; im-
      proving the administration of justice; and furthering intergovernmental relations.

27P .. TRADE POLICY TOWARD LOW-INCOME COUNTRIES $1.50   _____
      Presents 12 recommendations concerning trade policies of the high-income countries
      toward the low-income countries. It includes specific proposals to help increase the
      export earnings of the world's developing regions.

26P .. A FISCAL PROGRAM FOR A BALANCED FEDERALISM $1.00   _____
      Considers what should be done by state and local governments to increase their
      fiscal authority and responsibility to meet the rapidly growing demand for public
      services.

24P .. HOW LOW INCOME COUNTRIES CAN ADVANCE THEIR OWN GROWTH $1.50   _____
      Describes the internal aspects of economic development and the essential require-
      ments for achieving sustained high rates of growth in per capita income, drawn from
      the experience of the low income countries.

23P .. MODERNIZING LOCAL GOVERNMENT $1.00   _____
      A hard-hitting analysis of the need for better local government so that towns,
      counties, cities, and suburbs can cope with present day conditions — with a series
      of recommendations for structural changes that would alleviate the severe and
      increasing social, political, and financial strains on these governments.

22P .. A BETTER BALANCE IN FEDERAL TAXES ON BUSINESS   75¢   _____
      This statement urges consideration of a federal value-added tax on business. This
      tax should substitute for a part of the corporate income tax as soon as revenue
      conditions permit.

21P .. BUDGETING FOR NATIONAL OBJECTIVES $1.00   _____
      The federal budgeting process should be used as the essential instrument for defin-
      ing and achieving national purposes. Both executive and legislative branches can
      employ the budget more effectively to reach rational policy and program decisions
      and to ensure efficient management.

15P .. EDUCATING TOMORROW'S MANAGERS $1.00   _____
      Seeks to increase public understanding of the functions of business schools and
      departments in American colleges and universities.

14P .. IMPROVING EXECUTIVE MANAGEMENT IN THE FEDERAL GOVERNMENT $1.50   _____
      Calls for major reforms in the selection, development, compensation, and utiliza-
      tion of the 8600 career executives and professionals.

9P .. ECONOMIC LITERACY FOR AMERICANS   75¢   _____
      An objective appraisal of the present state of economic literacy in the United States
      and a realistic plan for improving it.

1P .. ECONOMIC GROWTH IN THE UNITED STATES $1.00   _____
      A Statement on National Policy by the Research and Policy Committee first issued
      in 1958; updated and reissued by the Program Committee, October 1969.

Quantity discounts: 10-24 copies—10%, 25-49 copies—15%, 50-99 copies—20%, 100-249 copies—30%

NOTE TO EDUCATORS: Instructors in colleges and universities may obtain
for teaching purposes up to 5 copies of each Statement on National Policy free
of charge. For more than 5 copies, an educational discount of 20% will apply.

☐ I am enclosing $............................. for the copies ordered above.

☐ Please bill me. *(Remit for orders under $10.00)*

DO YOU WANT ALL CED PUBLICATIONS WHEN ISSUED?

☐ I would like to obtain all CED publications as soon as they are issued. Please send
me information about the CED Reader Forum subscription plan.

☐ Please send me newest list of publications.

☐ Please send me newest list of CED international library items published by CED
counterpart organizations in Europe, Japan, Latin America, and Australia.

Name..

Address..

City...State...Zip.........................

    ☐ Businessman   ☐ Educator   ☐ Professional

TEAR OUT ON DOTTED LINE AND MAIL IN ENVELOPE TO CED